**Björn Krüger**

**Synthesizing Human Motions**

Björn Krüger

# Synthesizing Human Motions

## Various Data-Driven Approaches

Südwestdeutscher Verlag für Hochschulschriften

**Impressum / Imprint**
Bibliografische Information der Deutschen Nationalbibliothek: Die Deutsche Nationalbibliothek verzeichnet diese Publikation in der Deutschen Nationalbibliografie; detaillierte bibliografische Daten sind im Internet über http://dnb.d-nb.de abrufbar.
Alle in diesem Buch genannten Marken und Produktnamen unterliegen warenzeichen-, marken- oder patentrechtlichem Schutz bzw. sind Warenzeichen oder eingetragene Warenzeichen der jeweiligen Inhaber. Die Wiedergabe von Marken, Produktnamen, Gebrauchsnamen, Handelsnamen, Warenbezeichnungen u.s.w. in diesem Werk berechtigt auch ohne besondere Kennzeichnung nicht zu der Annahme, dass solche Namen im Sinne der Warenzeichen- und Markenschutzgesetzgebung als frei zu betrachten wären und daher von jedermann benutzt werden dürften.

Bibliographic information published by the Deutsche Nationalbibliothek: The Deutsche Nationalbibliothek lists this publication in the Deutsche Nationalbibliografie; detailed bibliographic data are available in the Internet at http://dnb.d-nb.de.
Any brand names and product names mentioned in this book are subject to trademark, brand or patent protection and are trademarks or registered trademarks of their respective holders. The use of brand names, product names, common names, trade names, product descriptions etc. even without a particular marking in this works is in no way to be construed to mean that such names may be regarded as unrestricted in respect of trademark and brand protection legislation and could thus be used by anyone.

Coverbild / Cover image: www.ingimage.com

Verlag / Publisher:
Südwestdeutscher Verlag für Hochschulschriften
ist ein Imprint der / is a trademark of
AV Akademikerverlag GmbH & Co. KG
Heinrich-Böcking-Str. 6-8, 66121 Saarbrücken, Deutschland / Germany
Email: info@svh-verlag.de

Herstellung: siehe letzte Seite /
Printed at: see last page
**ISBN: 978-3-8381-3029-3**

Zugl. / Approved by: Bonn, Universität, Diss., 2012

Copyright © 2012 AV Akademikerverlag GmbH & Co. KG
Alle Rechte vorbehalten. / All rights reserved. Saarbrücken 2012

# Abstract

In this work various data-driven methods for the synthesis of natural human full body motions are presented. My research in this area was based on the following fundamental questions: Suppose we have all the motion capture data ever recorded, how could we use them? What benefits do they offer us? Which applications can arise?

In fact, most of the motion capture data recorded are used for one specific project only and never reused although all these motion data contain valuable information about how human motions look like. To be able to handle a large amount of motion capture data I developed two basic techniques: A method for fast similarity search of single poses and motion sequences and a method for automatic annotation of motion capture data. Based on these two basic techniques three different methods of motion synthesis have been developed.

In the first approach, tensor based multilinear representations are constructed from annotated motion sequences. As will be shown this representation is especially suitable for motion synthesis.

In the second approach, given motion sequences are enhanced with respect to missing degrees of freedom using a technique for motion texturing. Here, similar motions are retrieved efficiently from the database, using a novel technique for fast similarity search. This fast motion retrieval was identified as the essential step to use the database as prior-knowledge to drive the synthesis process.

Finally a technique for motion synthesis from sparse key frames is introduced. Employing the search algorithm again, a so called motion graph, a structure for motion synthesis is computed on the fly. The result of this synthesis is then refined by the motion texturing approach.

All techniques and algorithms are tested and evaluated on the two largest freely available motion capture databases.

# Contents

**1 Introduction**     7
    1.1 Organization . . . . . . . . . . . . . . . . . . . . . . . . . 8

**2 Fast Similarity Searches**     9
    2.1 Introduction . . . . . . . . . . . . . . . . . . . . . . . . . . 10
       2.1.1 Our contributions . . . . . . . . . . . . . . . . . . . 11
    2.2 Related Work . . . . . . . . . . . . . . . . . . . . . . . . . 12
       2.2.1 Nearest-neighbor-search for human motion . . . . . . . . . 12
       2.2.2 Low and medium dimensional feature sets for human motion    13
    2.3 Feature Sets . . . . . . . . . . . . . . . . . . . . . . . . . 13
       2.3.1 Previously described distance measures and feature sets for human motions . . . . . . . . . . . . . . . . . . . . . 14
       2.3.2 Devising novel medium dimensional feature sets . . . . . . 15
       2.3.3 Comparing feature sets . . . . . . . . . . . . . . . . . 16
    2.4 Motion Matching . . . . . . . . . . . . . . . . . . . . . . . 25
       2.4.1 A novel approach to fast global motion matching . . . . . . 26
       2.4.2 Comparing the global motion matching for different feature sets . . . . . . . . . . . . . . . . . . . . . . . . . . . 28
    2.5 Applications . . . . . . . . . . . . . . . . . . . . . . . . . 30
       2.5.1 Numerical and Logical Similarity Searches . . . . . . . . . 30
       2.5.2 Reconstruction of Motions from Few Markers . . . . . . . . 31
       2.5.3 Fast Fat Graphs . . . . . . . . . . . . . . . . . . . . 33

## CONTENTS

    2.6    Including Physics . . . . . . . . . . . . . . . . . . . . . 34
            2.6.1    Physics-based feature sets . . . . . . . . . . . . 34
            2.6.2    Experiments and Results . . . . . . . . . . . . . 36
    2.7    Online Method . . . . . . . . . . . . . . . . . . . . . . . 37
    2.8    Conclusion and Future Work . . . . . . . . . . . . . . . 38

**3 Motion Annotation**      **43**
    3.1    Related Work . . . . . . . . . . . . . . . . . . . . . . . 45
    3.2    Annotation via Class Motion Templates . . . . . . . . . 46
            3.2.1    Motion Templates . . . . . . . . . . . . . . . . . 46
            3.2.2    Annotation procedure . . . . . . . . . . . . . . . 47
            3.2.3    Experiments . . . . . . . . . . . . . . . . . . . . 49
    3.3    Parametrization via Class Motion Tensors . . . . . . . . 52
            3.3.1    Motion Tensors . . . . . . . . . . . . . . . . . . 53
            3.3.2    Parametrization Procedure . . . . . . . . . . . . 55
            3.3.3    Experiments . . . . . . . . . . . . . . . . . . . . 56
    3.4    Conclusion . . . . . . . . . . . . . . . . . . . . . . . . . 58

**4 Motion Synthesis**      **61**
    4.1    Multilinear Representation . . . . . . . . . . . . . . . . 62
            4.1.1    Introduction . . . . . . . . . . . . . . . . . . . . 62
            4.1.2    Multilinear Algebra . . . . . . . . . . . . . . . . 65
            4.1.3    Motion Warping . . . . . . . . . . . . . . . . . 68
            4.1.4    Experimental Results . . . . . . . . . . . . . . . 73
            4.1.5    Conclusion and Future Work . . . . . . . . . . . 81
    4.2    Data-driven Texturing of Human Motions . . . . . . . . 86
            4.2.1    Introduction . . . . . . . . . . . . . . . . . . . . 86
            4.2.2    Overview . . . . . . . . . . . . . . . . . . . . . 86
            4.2.3    Prior Terms . . . . . . . . . . . . . . . . . . . . 88
            4.2.4    Optimization procedure . . . . . . . . . . . . . 90
            4.2.5    Results . . . . . . . . . . . . . . . . . . . . . . . 91
            4.2.6    Conclusion and Future Work . . . . . . . . . . . 93

|  |  |  |  |
|---|---|---|---|
| | 4.3 | Dynamic Motion Graphs | 94 |
| | | 4.3.1 Related Work | 95 |
| | | 4.3.2 Overview | 97 |
| | | 4.3.3 Motion Graph Construction | 97 |
| | | 4.3.4 Cleaning the Intermediate Result | 102 |
| | | 4.3.5 Results | 103 |
| | | 4.3.6 Conclusion and Future Work | 107 |
| **5** | **Conclusion and Future Work** | | **113** |
| | 5.1 | Conclusion | 113 |
| | 5.2 | Future Work | 114 |
| **Bibliography** | | | **115** |

*"If I could see something—*
*You can see anything you want boy.*
*If I could be someone—*
*You can be anyone, celebrate boy.*
*If I could do something—*
*Well you can do something,*
*If I could do anything—*
*Well can you do something out of this world?"*

Supertramp – Dreamer

# 1

# Introduction

Motion capturing has become a standard technique in computer animation. A wide variety of motion capture systems are available: Starting from consumer electronics like Microsoft Kinect up to professional systems like Vicon MX or Giant. Professional motion capture systems enable us to track and record human motions at high spatial and temporal resolutions. The resulting 3D motion capture data are used for motion analysis in fields such as sports sciences, biomechanics, medical rehabilitation, or computer vision, and in particular for motion synthesis in data-driven computer animation.

In all areas mentioned the demand for synthetic motion data increases: There are more and more films produced that are totally or at least partially based on animated characters. At the same time the percentage of animated scenes increases, while the production time of films is getting shorter. Medical applications employ motion capture data to document and analyze the recovery of patients. In the sports area motion capture systems are used not only in sport sciences, but also in popular sports.

CHAPTER 1. INTRODUCTION

The display of these motions, which were recorded only in part with a few sensors, and the recording of which may contain gaps, is gaining importance. In computer games, virtual characters are becoming increasingly important, too. The gamers will increasingly interact with virtual characters. Therefore virtual characters must be able to react quickly, without acting unnaturally.

Today, in all these applications, the use of pre-recorded motion data only plays a minor role. If one wants to extend utilization of all these motion data, fast searching techniques are urgently needed. Time-consuming search is not acceptable in interactive or even real-time scenarios. For this reason I introduce a fast query by example searching technique that scales well to huge motion capture databases. If the stored motion capture data have to be structured, my motion annotation technique adds semantical information to the motion capture data. This semantical information can be used to improve keyword based motion retrieval techniques.

Based on these searching and annotation algorithms I develop new techniques for the synthesis of human motions. The main goal of these techniques for motion synthesis is to create natural full body animations that are not restricted to a small set of motion classes and can be adapted to the requirements of the applications mentioned above.

## 1.1 Organization

The remainder of the thesis is organized as follows: In Chapter 2 we introduce our fast searching technique for motion capture data and show its efficiency in different applications. Chapter 3 describes a technique for annotation of motion data based on two layers. Based on these frameworks three different techniques for motion synthesis are presented in Chapter 4. Finally, we close the thesis with a conclusion and proposals for future research activities.

*"I remember doing the time warp*
*Drinking those moments when*
*The blackness would hit me*
*and the void would be calling*
*Let's do the time warp again...*
*Let's do the time warp again!"*

Rocky Horror Picture Show

# 2

# Fast Similarity Searches in Motion Capture Databases

Fast searching of content in large motion databases is essential for efficient motion analysis and synthesis. In this work we demonstrate that identifying locally similar regions in human motion data can be practical even for huge databases, if medium-dimensional (15 to 90 dimensional) feature sets are used for kd-tree-based nearest-neighbor-searches. On the basis of kd-tree-based local neighborhood searches we devise a novel fast method for *global* similarity searches. We show that knn-searches can be used efficiently within the problems of (a) "numerical and logical similarity searches", (b) reconstruction of motions from sparse marker sets, and (c) building so called "fat graphs", tasks for which previously algorithms with preprocessing time quadratic in the size of the database and thus only applicable to small collections of motions had been presented. We test our techniques on the two largest freely available motion capture databases, the CMU and HDM05 motion databases comprising more than 750 minutes of motion capture data proving that our approach is not only theoretically applicable but also solves the problem of fast similarity searches in huge motion databases in practice.

## 2.1 Introduction

Searching for similar motion segments is of central importance for data driven approaches of motion synthesis and content-based retrieval of motion data. Whereas efficient indexing techniques being linear in the size of the motion database have been described, for the problem of finding logically similar motions, methods such as neighbor graphs or similarity matrices have been used for tasks requiring numerically similar motions. These however require a preprocessing time quadratic in the size of the motion capture database in use and are therefore impractical for larger databases.

Due to the dimensionality of motion capture data and the "curse of dimensionality" of search structures such as BSP-trees or kd-trees [BBK01] these had not been applied for similarity searches of motions, as was succinctly expressed by [KG04] (format of references adapted to our references):

> "One challenge in finding matches is that individual frames are high-dimensional objects with non-Euclidean distance metrics [KGP02, LCR+02]. As a result, traditional methods for organizing the data into a spatial hierarchy (such as a BSP-tree) can not be directly applied [BBK01]."

In contrast to kd-trees, which speed up searches using Euclidean distance metrics, R-trees, which efficiently speed up searches in $L_1$ norms, have already been used in the context of motion data by [KPZ+04].

2.1. INTRODUCTION

## 2.1.1 Our contributions

**Devising feature sets for fast similarity searches**

In this chapter we describe and analyze medium dimensional feature sets for human motions (in general 15 to 90 dimensional ones). These can be used with naturally occurring Euclidean distance measures in standard spatial data structures—specifically kd-trees—to perform fast exact and approximate similarity searches in large motion capture databases for various purposes.

**Analyzing different distance measures**

We systematically compare previously-described distance measures with each other and with those induced by our feature sets. This comparison is done locally, i.e. on single frames, as well as globally, i.e. on motion segments, on the basis of the CMU [Car04] and HDM05 [MRC[+]07] databases.

**Expanding pose matching to motion matching**

On the basis of the fast kd-tree-based pose matching and local motion matching we devise a novel fast method for global motion matching. For a motion database of size $n$ and a query sequence $Q$ consisting of $m$ frames using local $k$-nearest-neighbor-searches the overall complexity of the global similarity search is $O(km \log n)$, with $m \ll n$ and $k \ll n$.

Moreover, we show that distances on neighboring motion segments (parameterized by a local distance measure) induced by our novel technique are in general equivalent to the similarity measures computed by *dynamic time warping* (DTW) parameterized by the same local distance measure. Thus, our method can be used as a fast alternative to subsequence DTW-based alignment.

**Demonstrating the usability of fast similarity searches for different applications**

We apply fast similarity searches of time complexity $O(n \log n)$ in the size of a database $n$ to the problems of "numerical similarity searches", reconstruction of motions from sparse marker sets, and building so called "fat graphs", tasks for which previous algorithms with quadratic preprocessing time have been proposed.

## 2.2 Related Work

### 2.2.1 Nearest-neighbor-search for human motion

Chai and Hodgins [CH05] use a neighbor graph in a preprocessing step on a motion database allowing fast nearest-neighbor-search. However, the preprocessing step requires time quadratic to the size of the database and thus does not scale well to larger motion databases.

Kovar and Gleicher [KG04] perform numerical and "logical" similarity searches on collections of motion capture data. They build so called "match webs" on dense distance matrices, thus requiring a preprocessing time quadratic in the size of motion capture data.

The problem of finding short motion segments that are similar to a given one is also of central importance when synthetic transitions between motions are generated. Here the concept of "motion graphs" [KGP02, SO06, HG07, SH07, MP07] has become a central tool. However, in all these approaches the generation of the various variants requires an effort quadratic to the size of the motion database and thus cannot be used for large collections of motions.

Müller et al. [MRC05] use binary geometric features and index structures to address the problem of content-based retrieval on large motion databases. Whereas the binary geometric features are well suited for defining notions of logical similarity of motions and for coming up with "motion templates" [MR06], they are not suitable in contexts requiring close numerical similarity of motions.

The use of spatial search structures is well established for multi-media databases [BBK01]. Also a "generic multimedia indexing approach" (GEMINI) [Fal96] has been widely used for multi-media applications for more than a decade. However, the crucial step is to have suitable low-dimensional feature sets that can be used with an efficient spatial access method. In the context of motion data, its use and the use of R-trees are abstractly discussed in [FHP07], and Keogh et al. [KPZ+04] use R-trees for searching lower and upper bounds, which naturally yield $L_1$ norms, efficiently. However, prior to our own work presented here we are not aware of any practical attempts to define low- or medium-dimensional feature sets for human motion data and using them both for efficient spatial access methods for Euclidean distance measures and for fast similarity searches in large motion databases.

The techniques of locality sensitive hashing (LSH) [AI08] for fast approximate nearest-neighbor-search in high dimensions has recently been applied to the problem of mining "motion motifs" from medium-sized collections of motion data (of about 32 000 frames) [MYHW08].

### 2.2.2 Low and medium dimensional feature sets for human motion

For small databases it is well known that human motions have very good 7–10 dimensional approximations [SHP04, EMMT04, CH05], which can be obtained by simple techniques like PCA (principal component analysis) on the angular skeleton representation. However, for large heterogenous databases such low-dimensional approximations are less accurate [CH05] and higher dimensional feature sets are required. Beaudoin et al. [BCPP08] use 18 dimensional PCA approximations of joint angle data.

The suitability of our medium dimensional geometric features for describing human poses is closely related to the well known analysis of the inverse kinematics problem for anthropomorphic limbs [TGB00]. An evaluation of different distance metrics for blending purposes is given in [BE09].

## 2.3 Feature Sets for Fast Similarity Searches of Human Motions

In order to compare our newly-devised feature sets with existing ones, we will first review various distance measures for human motions and feature sets (with induced

*Figure 2.1: Visualizations of the 256 nearest neighbors for 9 exemplary poses. All results were computed using feature set $\mathcal{F}_E^{15}$ on the union of CMU and HDM05 motion database. The positions of the wrist and ankle joints as well as head joints are visualized for the nearest neighbors (with color fading out with increasing distance). In all cases the nearest neighbors have been computed in a few milliseconds within databases containing more than 750 minutes of motion capture data.*

distance measures) that have been described in the literature. Specifically we will fix the notations for them.

### 2.3.1 Previously described distance measures and feature sets for human motions

There are purely pose-based distance measures such as the one measuring distances on joint angles [CH05]. As the distance measure depends on the encoding of the joint angles, e.g., whether quaternion-based representations or Euler angle-based representations are used, we denote the former one by $\mathcal{D}_{quat}$ and the latter one by $\mathcal{D}_{euler}$. More specifically, the Euler angles in the standard asf/amc representation of the mocap data will be used. PCA-based compression of pose-based feature sets [SHP04, CH05, BCPP08] will be denoted by $\mathcal{F}_{pca}^{pn}$. Here, $n$ means the number of principal components on joint positions in body frame—pre-computed on a fixed database, which will be chosen to be the entire HDM05 database in all our experiments ($n$ dimensions).

In order to describe not only the properties of a pose statically but also to encode the kinematic properties of a motion sequence in the feature set of a frame, Kovar and Gleicher [KG04] introduced a point cloud distance measure on a normalized window of the previous and subsequent $n/2$ poses. In the following chapters this distance measure will be denoted by $\mathcal{D}_{pcn}$.

## 2.3. FEATURE SETS

In [LCR+02] the authors describe a cost function to determine transition points in motion streams, defining the distance between two frames as the sum of weighted differences of joint angles as well as of joint velocities. Whereas Lee et al. [LCR+02] propose a set of weights containing one and zero only—setting the weights to one for the shoulders, elbows, hips, knees, pelvis, and spine and setting all others to zero—Wang and Bodenheimer [WB03, WB08] use a refined cost metric. By using motion capture data to determine optimal values for all weights that modify the transition costs, they reason that only certain joints are considered important and thus are associated with non-zero weights–right and left hip, right and left knee, right and left shoulder, right and left elbow. The resulting distance measure, which is based on the optimized weights, will also be investigated and in the following chapters will be denoted as $\mathcal{D}_{wb}$.

### 2.3.2 Devising novel medium dimensional feature sets

We will devise several medium dimensional feature sets of increasing dimensionality: we define frame-based geometric feature sets that can be extended to local feature sets on frame windows.

**Frame-based feature sets**

For our geometric features we use normalized root positions and orientations, as is the standard technique for features of human motion data [KG04, CH05, AFO03]. Our primary feature set

$\mathcal{F}_E^{15}$ consists of the positions of 4 end-effectors and head.

This 15-dimensional feature set is motivated by the following considerations:

- As is well known the geometry of anthropomorphic limbs is fully determined by the positions of the end-effectors, their orientation, and one single additional scalar quantity—the so called "swivel angle" [TGB00]. Moreover, the corresponding inverse kinematics problem can be solved very efficiently by using analytic solutions [TGB00, HJBC05].

# CHAPTER 2. FAST SIMILARITY SEARCHES

- For typical human motions the orientations of the end-effectors are statistically quite dependent on the end-effector positions, as are the values of the swivel angles, so that the positions of the arms and legs should be well determined.

- Given the positions of the legs, the arms, and the head as well as the position of the root (due to normalization) there should be little variability in body positions.

For the sake of comparison (and for statistically validating the claims made above), we also use the following two pose-based geometric feature sets:

$\mathcal{F}_E^{30}$ Positions of 4 end-effectors, and head, as well as the 5 positions of the elbows, knees and one chest joint (30 dimensions).

$\mathcal{F}_E^{39}$ All features of $\mathcal{F}_E^{30}$; in addition position of the shoulders and one lower-back joint (39 dimensions).

**Feature sets on windows of frames**

Purely pose-based feature sets such as $\mathcal{F}_E^{15}$ give no information about the temporal evolution of a motion. In contrast, feature sets including several frames on a small window represent the local evolution in time. Based on this observation it is possible to extend every frame-based distance measure $\mathcal{F}^n$ of dimension $n$ to one on a window of $l$ frames $\mathcal{F}^{n \times l}$ of dimension $nl$. We will sample the windows sparsely, using only 3 or 5 frames on a window of fixed length 0.3 seconds—a value commonly used in the literature for the size of local motion windows. The resulting feature sets will be denoted by $\mathcal{F}_E^{15 \times 3}, \mathcal{F}_E^{15 \times 5}, \mathcal{F}_E^{30 \times 3}$, and $\mathcal{F}_E^{39 \times 3}$.

## 2.3.3 Comparing feature sets

**Pose based comparisons**

Our comparisons will be focused on feature sets designed to identify neighborhoods of a pose, because they are of main concern in the applications. As the search using

## 2.3. FEATURE SETS

*Table 2.1: Average computation times (in milliseconds) for searching 16 (256) nearest neighbors using various feature sets on motions of HDM05 database (380 813 frames at 30 Hz) and CMU database (1 038 388 frames at 30 Hz).*

| database | #NN | $\mathcal{F}_{pca}^{p8}$ | $\mathcal{F}_{pca}^{p16}$ | $\mathcal{F}_{pca}^{p25}$ | $\mathcal{F}_E^{15}$ | $\mathcal{F}_E^{30}$ | $\mathcal{F}_E^{39}$ | $\mathcal{F}_E^{15 \times 3}$ | $\mathcal{F}_E^{15 \times 5}$ | $\mathcal{F}_E^{30 \times 3}$ |
|---|---|---|---|---|---|---|---|---|---|---|
| HDM05 | 16 | 0.19 | 1.33 | 2.86 | 1.11 | 3.87 | 5.27 | 7.95 | 14.01 | 18.98 |
|  | 256 | 1.03 | 4.99 | 8.68 | 4.53 | 12.50 | 16.37 | 23.70 | 36.22 | 46.71 |
| CMU | 16 | 0.25 | 2.15 | 5.37 | 1.65 | 6.37 | 8.71 | 20.62 | 37.08 | 55.59 |
|  | 256 | 1.35 | 8.97 | 18.10 | 7.36 | 24.12 | 31.68 | 60.23 | 96.55 | 136.29 |

kd-trees can be done efficiently for all of our feature sets, cf. Table 2.1, it is possible to do such comparisons systematically for large motion capture databases. For all of our experiments $k$-nearest-neighbor-searches were performed using the ANN library [MA06].

In Table 2.1 the computation times for the previously defined feature sets searching for the nearest 16 resp. 256 nearest neighbors on the HDM05 database (380 813 frames at 30 Hz) and CMU database (1 038 388 frames at 30 Hz) are given for exact ($\epsilon = 0$) nearest-neighbor-searches.

Our frame-based (15 to 39 dimensional) feature sets allow very fast nearest-neighbor-searches and show the expected good scaling from a database consisting of 380 813 to one consisting of 1 038 388 frames.

The running times of the previously described feature sets had the expected behavior according to their dimensionalities.

For the windowed feature sets (of dimension 45 to 90) the search times are about one order of magnitude higher than for the ones based on single frames—thus, being much better than worst case theoretical considerations predict. Thus, even if these feature sets do not in general fulfill hard real time requirements on current PCs for large motion databases, they are nevertheless practical for many applications.

However, as will be shown below, the use of higher-dimensional feature sets gives little or no advantage over the use of lower dimensional ones—specifically the simple feature set $\mathcal{F}_E^{15}$.

**Pose-based comparisons on a small sample database**

In Figure 2.4 the correlations between the previously-described feature sets and distance measures are given. In order to compare the distance measures we use Spear-

## CHAPTER 2. FAST SIMILARITY SEARCHES

man's rank correlation coefficient $\rho$ [MW03], which is a robust measure with respect to commonly used slight but non-linear variations of the distance measures. This overall comparison is based on a small sample database as for the high-dimensional distance measures we do not have a fast nearest-neighbor-search method.

Note that the matrices are *not symmetric*, as we perform the correlations on the nearest neighbors according to the feature set given on the vertical axis. This asymmetric behavior is especially prominent for $\mathcal{D}_{quat}$ in comparison to $\mathcal{D}_{euler}$ and the frame-based feature sets with their counterparts involving 3 or 5 frames. These observations are easily explainable: if the distance on angular representations given by Euler angles are similar, so are the ones given by quaternions, whereas similar quaternion-based distances might result in bigger differences in Euler angles (especially in "near gimbal lock" configurations). And if the distances according to a feature set involving $l$ frames are similar, then so are the ones involving single frames, whereas vice versa, the similarities in one frame, involving static information only might result in fewer similar measures based on $l$ frames.

Nevertheless, there is also a rather high rank correlation between $\mathcal{D}_{pc1}$ and $\mathcal{D}_{pc11}$, and frame-based feature sets and their counterparts involving 3 or 5 frames. Moreover, the distance measures based on $\mathcal{F}_E^{15\times3}$ and $\mathcal{F}_E^{15\times5}$ are *very highly correlated*: using 5 frame samples instead of 3 gives little additional information, so that the lower dimensional feature set can be used yielding lower computation times.

The distance measures based on $\mathcal{F}_E^{30}$ and $\mathcal{F}_E^{39}$ are *very highly correlated*: using the normalized root position, the head position and the ones of arms and legs there is almost no additional statistical variety in the body positions. Also $\mathcal{F}_E^{15}$ and $\mathcal{F}_E^{30}$ are highly correlated: there is already a very high statistical determination of the arm and leg positions from their end-effector positions.

Whereas $\mathcal{F}_{pca}^{p16}$ is comparable in general to other feature sets, the use of only 8 dimensions in $\mathcal{F}_{pca}^{p8}$ is connected with a strong loss in correlation. The feature sets $\mathcal{F}_{pca}^{p16}$ and $\mathcal{F}_{pca}^{p25}$ are very highly correlated indicating that most information on the motions is already contained in the first 16 principal components.

## 2.3. FEATURE SETS

**Pose-based comparisons on large databases**

Using our fast similarity searches we can extend the correlation analysis to large motion capture databases for the cases in which the correlations are computed on nearest neighbors defined by one of the medium-dimensional feature sets.

In general the findings are similar to the ones on the small sample database described above. Especially, the correlations between $\mathcal{F}_E^{15\times3}$, $\mathcal{F}_E^{15\times5}$, and $\mathcal{F}_E^{30\times3}$ are still very high, and these are highly correlated to $\mathcal{D}_{pcl1}$. The single-frame-based feature sets $\mathcal{F}_E^{30}$ and $\mathcal{F}_E^{39}$ are still *very highly correlated*, and there is still a high correlation to $\mathcal{F}_E^{15}$. Also a rather high correlation to $\mathcal{D}_{pcl}$ exists.

On this larger database the correlations to the PCA-based feature sets are somewhat lower, and so are the correlations between the single frame based feature sets and their counterparts involving 3 or 5 frames. Figure 2.5 shows all rank correlations corresponding to pose-based comparisons on a large database.

**Root normalizations**

In the HDM05 database there are several actions that were performed on a stair rather than on flat ground. Such motions tend to be numerically very different from other ground plane motions if standard 2D root normalization—restricting the translations to the ground plane—is applied. To avoid misalignment we instead use a full 3D normalization of the root position for all of our new feature sets. Please note that—following the definitions found in the literature—only 2D translations have been previously regarded for $\mathcal{D}_{pcl}$ and $\mathcal{D}_{pcl1}$. Hence, not very surprisingly, the rank correlations of $\mathcal{F}_E^{15}$ and $\mathcal{D}_{pcl}$ increase from 0.55 to 0.62 (for 512 NN) if our feature sets are computed under standard 2D normalization, cf. Figure 2.5.

Of course, we can easily define variants of our feature sets for which only 2D normalizations of the root positions are considered (or alternatively allow 3D translations in variants of $\mathcal{D}_{pcl}$ or $\mathcal{D}_{pcl1}$). It is certainly application specific whether the 2D or 3D normalizations of the root positions should be used. As we presume that the 3D normalizations should be more common, we have used those for our comparisons.

## CHAPTER 2. FAST SIMILARITY SEARCHES

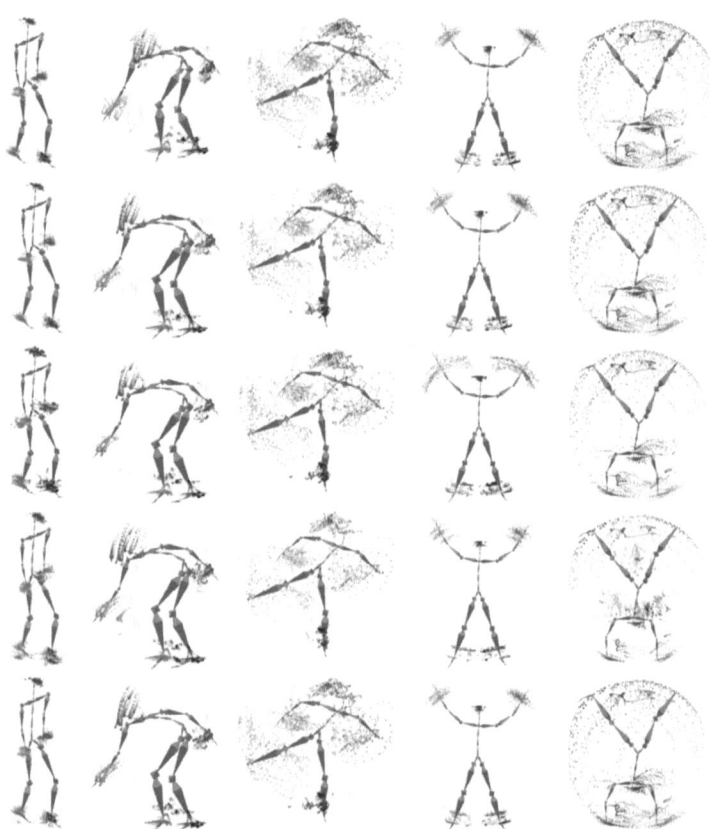

*Figure 2.2:* Visualization of the neighborhood of five poses from different motion classes (from left to right: walk, grab floor, kick, jumping jack and cartwheel) with respect to various feature sets (top down: $\mathcal{F}_E^{15}, \mathcal{F}_E^{30}, \mathcal{F}_E^{15\times 3}, \mathcal{F}_{pca}^{p8}$ and $\mathcal{F}_{pca}^{p16}$).

## 2.3. FEATURE SETS

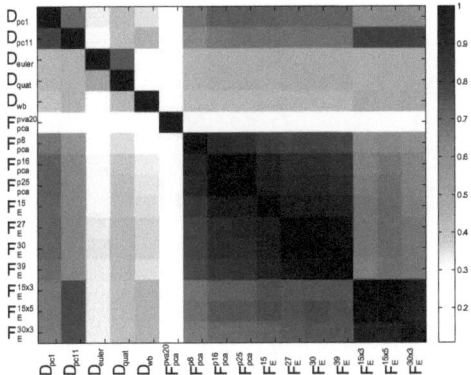

*Figure 2.3: Rank correlations between various distance measures and feature sets on an example database based on 76 motion clips taken from the HDM05 database: Average values for 1024 random samples choosing 512 nearest neighbors according to the feature set given in the vertical axis with the distance measure given in the horizontal axis.*

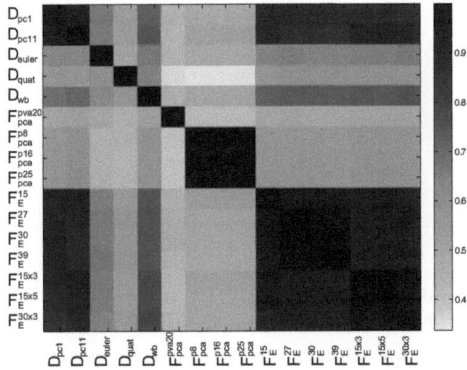

*Figure 2.4: Rank correlations for DTW-induced global distance measures on motion segments (8 NN) taken from an example database based on 76 motion clips taken from the HDM05 database: Average values for all 76 motion clips choosing 8 nearest neighbors (restricted to the set of 76 cut motion clips) according to the feature set on the vertical axis. The distances between all motion clips were computed by DTW on the distance measures on the horizontal axis as well as on the vertical axis.*

## CHAPTER 2. FAST SIMILARITY SEARCHES

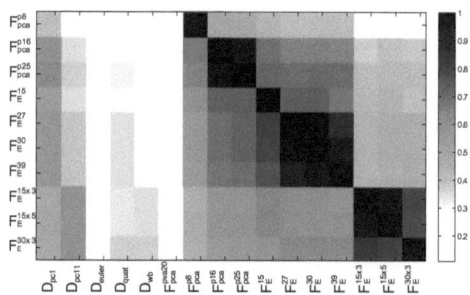

Figure 2.5: Rank correlations between various distance measures and feature sets on the entire HDM05 database: Rank correlations for local distance measures (512 NN). Average values for 1024 random samples choosing 512 nearest neighbors according to the feature set given in the vertical axis with the distance measure given in the horizontal axis.

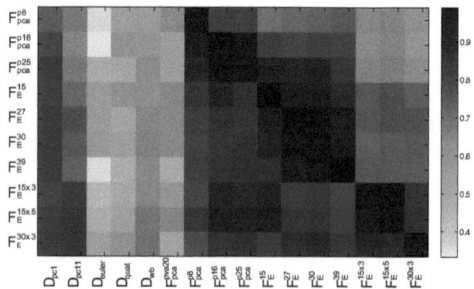

Figure 2.6: Rank correlations between various distance measures and feature sets on the entire HDM05 database: Rank correlations for induced global distances according to the fast neighborhood search versus DTW-induced global distance measures on motion segments. Average values for 76 motion clips choosing 8 nearest neighbors found by the fast global neighborhood search out of the entire HDM05 database according to the feature set on the vertical axis. For feature sets on the vertical axis the global distances according to the fast neighborhood search were ranked against the global distances computed by DTW on the distance measures on the horizontal axis.

## 2.3. FEATURE SETS

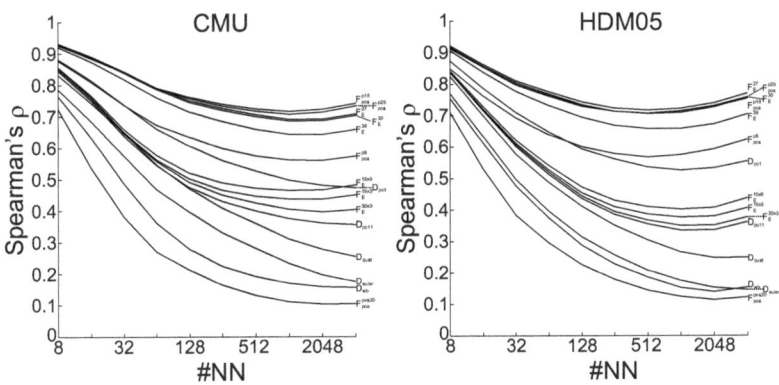

*Figure 2.7: Rank correlations between feature set $\mathcal{F}_E^{15}$ and other feature sets on the entire CMU and HDM05 databases depending on the number of nearest neighbors involved.*

**Dependency on number of nearest neighbors involved**

The rank correlation coefficients depend on the number of nearest neighbors involved. In Figure 2.7 the rank correlations between feature set $\mathcal{F}_E^{15}$ and other feature sets on the entire HDM05 and CMU databases depending on the number of nearest neighbors involved are given (for 8 to 4096 NN). The correlations depend on the number of nearest neighbors, decreasing in value for 8 to 512 NN staying in about the same level for 512 to 4096 NN. However, as can be seen from Figure 2.7 the differences of correlations between the different feature sets remain about the same. The computations on the HDM05 and CMU databases qualitatively show the same behavior. We have done corresponding computations for all of our feature sets with the same qualitative result for all of them.

**Motion segment based comparisons**

We now focus on comparisons between motion segments, based on several feature sets and distance measures. These comparisons show relationships between the definitions of similarity induced by the feature sets and distance measures.

As an example dataset we used 76 hand-cut motion sequences from the HDM05 database. This example dataset contains nine motion classes where at least eight motions of every class were available.

For direct comparison of the motion sequences we performed a dynamic time warping between each pair of 76 motion sequences for every feature set and distance measure. Based on this DTW-distances (accumulated pose distances along the warping path) we performed a ranking. As a result we obtained a ranked list of motions for each motion of the example dataset. Since the use of similar feature sets or distance measures should give similar rankings of the motion sequences, we computed rank correlations for the first eight motions of this ranking.

This rather small number is motivated by the consideration that we are concerned with the distance metrics on similar motions and not on very different ones (say a walking and a grasping motion)—and we know that at least eight motions of every class are available in the database.

In general the correlations are similar to the point-wise evaluations. There is a higher correlation for $\mathcal{D}_{wb}$ to almost all other distance measures and feature sets than for the point wise evaluation, whereas the correlations for the PCA-feature sets decrease. The correlations between our feature sets $\mathcal{F}_E^{15}$, $\mathcal{F}_E^{30}$, and $\mathcal{F}_E^{39}$ in between but especially to their counterparts involving several frames increase. The latter observation can be explained by the fact that for a point-wise evaluation the frame-based feature sets on the level of single frames *do not* distinguish directions of the motion in contrast to $\mathcal{F}_E^{15\times 3}$, $\mathcal{F}_E^{15\times 5}$, or $\mathcal{F}_E^{30\times 3}$, but nevertheless the warping paths are quite similar, cf. Figure 2.8.

**Motion segment based comparisons on large databases**

We could also perform motion segment-based comparisons on large databases using the fast global motion-matching methods described in Section 2.4.

The main differences to the evaluation on a small database are the higher correlations to the PCA-based feature sets. This finding might be explained by the fact that the PCA-based features are computed on the entire database, so that these perform better on random samples than on specifically-selected samples.

## Conclusions from the comparisons

As expected the low-dimensional feature sets $\mathcal{F}_E^{15}$ and the PCA-based feature sets allow the fastest nearest-neighbor searches. As the correlation of $\mathcal{F}_E^{15}$ to the higher-dimensional ones and to $\mathcal{D}_{pcI}$ as well as to $\mathcal{D}_{pcII}$ is higher than for $\mathcal{F}_{pca}^{p16}$ the former one should be preferred.

As $\mathcal{F}_E^{15}$ as a purely frame-based feature set does not distinguish directions of the motion in contrast to $\mathcal{F}_E^{15\times 3}$, there will be certain applications for which $\mathcal{F}_E^{15\times 3}$ should be used. However, we will show in Section 2.4 and Section 2.5 that for several applications, for which a priori one would suspect that including temporal information in a feature set plays a major role, nevertheless using the feature set $\mathcal{F}_E^{15}$ in the algorithms gives almost the same results as $\mathcal{F}_E^{15\times 3}$—but requires much shorter computation times.

So the simple feature set $\mathcal{F}_E^{15}$ seems to be the one of choice—especially for real-time applications.

## 2.4 From Pose Matching to Motion Matching

In many applications regarding analysis and synthesis of motions the problem of retrieving motion sequences within large unstructured motion databases, that are similar to a given query, is of central importance [KGP02, AFO03, KG04, SO06, HG07, SH07, MP07, BCPP08]. In the context of computer animation this problem was previously tackled by applying either *subsequence DTW* [Mül07] or *match web* [KG04] heuristics. Unfortunately, the above mentioned methods are computationally very costly. The construction of match webs in $O(n^2)$ and subsequence DTW has a complexity of $O(nm)$ where $m$ is the size of the query and $n$ is the number of frames included in the database.

In this section we are going to present a novel method in $O(m \log n)$ that gives similar results to subsequence DTW in practical scenarios and is more general and robust than match webs, since no ad-hoc heuristics are used. Our new approach is especially suitable for identifying closest matches to a given query. Practical applications demonstrating the efficiency of the method are given in Section 2.5.

## 2.4.1 A novel approach to fast global motion matching

In order to specify global motion-matching we follow the literature and define *a valid temporal alignment* of two motions as a continuous and monotonic mapping of poses [KG04]. For an optimal alignment of two motions we have to search for a sequence of consecutive frames (with ascending indices), which describes a discrete matching substitute to subsequence dynamic time warping.

To efficiently find similar motion segments included in a database (a sequential collection of motion clips indexed by frame) for a given query $Q$ we propose to use a novel technique, based on a "lazy neighborhood graph" (LNG). The novel method consists of four different key steps:

1. *preprocessing*, where a kd-tree is constructed,

2. *search*, for identifying local similarities of $Q$ and motions included in the database,

3. *graph construction*, for creating a lazy neighborhood graph,

4. *path search*, for finding global optimal alignments by solving a shortest path problem for this neighborhood graph.

**Preprocessing** As a preprocessing step we build a kd-tree for a motion database $D$ (of size $n$ frames) with respect to the feature set $\mathcal{F}$ to be considered.

For each query sequence $Q = [q_1 \cdots q_m]$ consisting of $m$ frames we proceed as follows:

**Search** Find nearest neighbors for each pose in $Q$ using fixed radius $k$-nearest-neighbor-search. The radius is given by $r$ and the maximum number of neighbors is limited by user defined parameter $k$. For each pose $q_i$ of the query a set $S(q_i)$ of poses that are similar according to $\mathcal{F}$ is retrieved in $O(k \log n)$. Thus, in total $km$ neighboring poses have to be stored, which requires $km$ space.

## 2.4. MOTION MATCHING

**Graph construction** Build a weighted and directed graph based on the sets $S$ by regarding each reported neighbor $h_j(q_i)$, $1 \leq j \leq k$ and $1 \leq i \leq m$, as a node and adding edges between nodes that form *valid continuations*. While many definitions of valid continuations are thinkable, we define them equivalent to the basic steps most commonly used in traversing DTW cost matrices, i.e. a diagonal, a horizontal and a vertical step. Formally spoken, this leads to edges between

- $h_j(q_i)$ and $h_l(q_{i+1})$ with $h_l(q_{i+1}) = h_j(q_i)+1$ (corresponding to the diagonal step),
- $h_j(q_i)$ and $h_l(q_i)$ with $h_l(q_i) = h_j(q_i) + 1$ (corresponding to the vertical step), and
- $h_j(q_i)$ and $h_l(q_{i+1})$ with $h_l(q_{i+1}) = h_j(q_i)$ (corresponding to the horizontal step).

Associating each edge with costs defined by the distance $d_j$ of the node they are pointing at—as reported by the kd-tree search—the task is now to find the paths with minimal costs that start in a node $h_j(q_1) \in S(q_1)$ and end up in a node $h_j(q_m) \in S(q_m)$.

**Path search** By adding one additional node to the graph and connecting it via edges to all $h_j(q_1) \in S(q_1)$ this task turns into a single-source shortest-path problem. Since the resulting graph is directed and acyclic and a topological ordering of its nodes—which means, whenever there is an edge from $x$ to $y$, the ordering visits $x$ before $y$—is directly given by construction, this problem can be solved in linear time [CLRS01] (Chapter 24.2).

This algorithm is parameterized by an arbitrary feature set $\mathcal{F}$. The global accumulated costs along the path define a global distance between the query motion and the motion segments found in the database. Thus, the retrieved motion segments can be ranked by their global distance according to the selected feature set $\mathcal{F}$. By this algorithm similar motion segments can be extracted in $O(km)$ time and the overall complexity for the similarity search is given by $O(km \log n)$.

CHAPTER 2. FAST SIMILARITY SEARCHES

The algorithm returns a best path for each match. These paths give a global optimal alignment between the query motion and the retrieved motion segments with respect to the local neighborhoods of each frame of the query motion.

The paths found by our method are equal to the paths found by subsequence dynamic time warping [Mül07] under the condition that all frames assigned to each other by subsequence DTW are in the neighborhood of the query motion. In tests on smaller databases such as the 76 cut motions this assumption was fulfilled in 100 % of the cases. For the tests on the entire HDM05 database the rank correlation between the global distances based on our approach and the global distances computed by dynamic time warping on the same feature sets was bigger than 0.99 for all feature sets (but not 1.0). Thus, for larger databases the assumption that all frames assigned to each other by subsequence DTW are in the neighborhood of the query motion fails in a few rare cases. In addition this issue becomes less relevant for applications in which only close matches are required. In such cases our approach can be seen to be an extremely efficient substitute for subsequence dynamic time warping.

*Remark.* Our algorithm was inspired by the trellis approach to extract motion motifs by Meng et al. [MYHW08]. The trellis approach as well as ours searches for local nearest neighbors parameterized by some distance measure. However, in the trellis approach only constant distances $d_j$ independent of the actual local costs are used. For that reason the original method fails to provide a temporal alignment of motion segments as it is achieved by our method. Moreover, there is no ranking of retrieved subsequences meaning that closest matches cannot be identified. Another serious drawback of the method described in [MYHW08] is the use of greedy strategies that in general fail to find global optimal alignments.

## 2.4.2 Comparing the global motion matching for different feature sets

Based on the algorithm described in the previous section we compare the results of our global matching with respect to various feature sets. For the sake of simplicity only a small sample database containing six steps of a left-turning walking motion,

## 2.4. MOTION MATCHING

starting with the right foot, is considered. A motion clip consisting of a two-step left-turning walking motion, starting with the right foot, is used as query.

As can be seen from the similarity matrices in Figure 2.8 the pose-based feature sets exhibit forward as well as backward diagonal structures for similar frames of query and database, as these pose-based feature sets do not incorporate velocity information and do not distinguish directly between forward and backward in motions (e.g., walking and running). Note that the windowed feature sets do not suffer from this issue. Nevertheless, the global motion-matching algorithm is able to identify the expected walking motions regardless of the feature set that was used for alignment. Note that the motion segments found by our algorithm are similar to the segments found by subsequence DTW based on $\mathcal{D}_{pcl}$. As the structure of the similarity matrices suggests, the task of finding warping paths is less constrained for the frame-based feature sets and thus more costly, since more potential alignments need to be investigated.

We did a more complete evaluation on the entire HDM05 database using 128 random motions of length 1 second and 128 random motions of length 3 seconds as queries. Searching alignments for windowed feature sets (excluding $k$-nearest-neighbor-search) was about 1.5 times faster than for frame-based ones. For the queries of length 1 second (3-sec) it took on average 0.03 seconds (0.08 seconds) to construct the alignments using exact nearest-neighbor-searches for the feature set $\mathcal{F}_{pca}^{p16}$. These experiments confirm that the asymptotic linear complexity in the length of the query of our algorithm also occurs in practice. Using approximate ($\epsilon = 0.1$) instead of exact nearest-neighbor-searches gave exactly the same results—with computation times for the kd-tree searches being about 10 % lower. When increasing epsilon to 0.5 about 99 % of the original alignments for the window-based feature sets were found. For the frame-based feature sets this rate dropped to 90 % to 95 % and the times for computing the alignment increased for approximate $k$-nearest-neighbor-search: 0.02 to 0.06 seconds on average for the 1 second queries (0.09 to 0.16 seconds for the 3 seconds queries). Note that the total timings for global motion-matching are dominated by the costs for $k$-nearest-neighbor-search (90%) cf. Table 2.1.

CHAPTER 2. FAST SIMILARITY SEARCHES

## 2.5 Applications

### 2.5.1 Numerical and Logical Similarity Searches

Kovar and Gleicher [KG04] presented a technique that allows numerical as well as "logical" similarity searches in motion databases. However, their technique does not scale to larger motion databases, as they have to compute a dense distance matrix of size $O(n^2)$, where $n$ is the number of frames in the database. Using the novel algorithm described in Section 2.4.1 we have a direct substitute for a "numerical similarity" search that scales well to huge motion databases. This technique allows for a substantial speedup of "logical similarity searches" originally proposed by Kovar and Gleicher [KG04]: use the set of found similar motion segments as queries for new iterations of similarity searches.

Not only do we avoid the preprocessing step of quadratic complexity to the size of the database $n$, but also for each query the cost of our method is only logarithmic to the size of the database instead of being linear as is the one from Kovar and Gleicher [KG04].

The basic properties of our numerical similarity search approach and results on a very small data sample were already presented in Section 2.4.2. A comparison of search results on a large motion database for different feature sets is given in Table 2.2.

As could be expected from the prototypical results on the very small database given in Figure 2.8, the results using the simple feature set $\mathcal{F}_E^{15}$ are the same or almost the same as for the higher dimensional feature sets $\mathcal{F}_E^{30}$, $\mathcal{F}_E^{39}$, $\mathcal{F}_E^{15 \times 3}$, $\mathcal{F}_E^{15 \times 5}$, and $\mathcal{F}_E^{30 \times 3}$ on the large database. Note that there are examples for which the simple feature sets return more similar motions than the higher-dimensional ones, and there are examples for which the higher dimensional ones return more similar motions than $\mathcal{F}_E^{15}$. Also the feature sets $\mathcal{F}_{pca}^{p16}$ and $\mathcal{F}_{pca}^{p25}$ yield similar search results, whereas $\mathcal{F}_{pca}^{p8}$ differs and also returns results not regarded as being similar by a human classification of the motions.

## 2.5. APPLICATIONS

*Table 2.2: Results for numerical similarity searches on the entire HDM05 database. A motion clip semantically classified to the motion class in the top row was used as query. The rows show the number of correct hits and in brackets the number of wrong hits that were not identified by our reference feature set $\mathcal{F}_E^{15}$, the number of false hits and finally in brackets the number of false hits not identified by $\mathcal{F}_E^{15}$.*

| | $\mathcal{F}_E^{15}$ | $\mathcal{F}_{pca}^{p8}$ | $\mathcal{F}_{pca}^{p16}$ | $\mathcal{F}_E^{30}$ | $\mathcal{F}_E^{15 \times 3}$ | $\mathcal{F}_E^{30 \times 3}$ |
|---|---|---|---|---|---|---|
| HDM_bk_kickRSide1Reps_007 | | | | | | |
| correct hits | 5(-) | 1(0) | 4(0) | 5(0) | 3(0) | 4(0) |
| wrong hits | 0(-) | 0(0) | 0(0) | 0(0) | 0(0) | 0(0) |
| HDM_tr_punchRSide1Reps_023 | | | | | | |
| correct hits | 6(-) | 4(0) | 6(0) | 8(2) | 6(3) | 9(6) |
| wrong hits | 0(-) | 0(0) | 0(0) | 0(0) | 0(0) | 2(2) |
| HDM_bk_skier1RepsLStart_011 | | | | | | |
| correct hits | 9(-) | 8(0) | 9(0) | 9(0) | 10(1) | 10(1) |
| wrong hits | 0(-) | 0(0) | 0(0) | 0(0) | 0(0) | 0(0) |

### 2.5.2 Reconstruction of Motions from Few Markers

Reconstructing motions from only a few markers is a challenging task that was recently tackled by Chai and Hodgins [CH05]. For their approach, identifying poses in a database as being similar to a given medium-dimensional control signal (sparse marker position data) is of central importance. The necessary pose-based nearest-neighbor-search was implemented by using a neighborhood graph, which requires a preprocessing effort quadratic to the size of the underlying motion capture database. Replacing the nearest-neighbor-search in a static graph by our fast kd-tree-based search method (on various of our feature sets) even orders of magnitude larger collections of motions become practical. Moreover, with kd-trees we can search around arbitrary, i.e. newly synthesized poses not included in the original database. Hence, we do not have to approximate the nearest-neighbor-search by using nearest neighbors of previously synthesized frames, as has to be done in [CH05].

In order to have ground truths for the quality of the reconstruction we performed the reconstructions on synthetic data obtained from test motions from the databases:

CHAPTER 2. FAST SIMILARITY SEARCHES

Table 2.3: Average (max) reconstruction errors (in cm per joint) for test motions from CMU and HDM05 database. We give the values for motions 86_01, 86_08, and 86_15 of CMU database, and for motions HDM_bk_01-01_01 and HDM_bk_02-01_01 of HDM05 database. The average error over the 15 motions in collection 86 of the CMU database is denoted as CMU_86_avg. We give the values for different databases for the pose priors. HDM: entire HDM05 database (possibly without test motion). $CMU^-$: CMU database without collection 86. CMU: entire CMU database (possibly without test motion). In all cases feature set $\mathcal{F}_E^{15}$ is used for the nearest-neighbor-search.

| motion | #frames | HDM | $CMU^-$ | CMU |
|---|---|---|---|---|
| CMU_86_01 | 1145 | 2.63 (6.47) | 2.06 (4.11) | 1.30 (3.42) |
| CMU_86_08 | 2302 | 3.06 (6.67) | 2.67 (6.95) | 1.96 (6.82) |
| CMU_86_15 | 1773 | 3.37 (6.41) | 2.64 (8.01) | 2.31 (5.88) |
| CMU_86_avg | 29040 | 2.79 (7.99) | 2.30 (5.58) | 1.74 (5.05) |
| HDM_bk_01-01_01 | 2571 | 1.33 (5.13) | 2.69 (5.04) | 2.70 (5.43) |
| HDM_bk_02-01_01 | 912 | 2.17 (6.45) | 3.23 (8.68) | 3.22 (8.65) |

the positions of the 4 end effectors, the head, and the root are taken as "marker positions" randomly disturbed within a range of 1mm (simulating measurement errors of an optical marker tracking).

The results given in Table 2.3 indicate that using the basic technique of Chai and Hodgins [CH05] a motion can be reconstructed reliably with 6 markers only, if large databases can be used to infer local statistics on motions (e.g., pose priors based on local linear models).

The quality of the reconstructions increases, if more motions related to the one to be reconstructed from sparse marker data are available—a result which is certainly expected but nevertheless shows the need to have fast similarity searches for motions on huge motion databases, a possibility opened by our method but not given by the original method of Chai and Hodgins [CH05].

As can be seen from the results shown in Table 2.4 the motion reconstruction procedure works quite well for all of the feature sets we have tested: it is enough to build a local linear model on a set of somewhat-related neighbors. Even those computed by a global 8 dimensional pca (as for feature $\mathcal{F}_{pca}^8$), which per se do not approximate the current motion segment well, are sufficient as a basis for the used local linear

## 2.5. APPLICATIONS

Table 2.4: *Average (max) reconstruction errors (in cm per joint) for a test motion using different feature sets for nearest-neighbor-searches. Entire CMU database without test motion was used for pose prior.*

| motion | $\mathcal{F}_E^{15}$ | $\mathcal{F}_{pca}^{p8}$ | $\mathcal{F}_{pca}^{p16}$ | $\mathcal{F}_{pca}^{p25}$ | $\mathcal{F}_E^{30}$ |
|---|---|---|---|---|---|
| CMU_86_03 | 1.66 | 1.71 | 1.49 | 1.41 | 1.35 |
|  | (4.73) | (5.09) | (5.25) | (4.80) | (4.55) |
| motion | $\mathcal{F}_E^{39}$ | $\mathcal{F}_E^{15 \times 3}$ | $\mathcal{F}_E^{15 \times 5}$ | $\mathcal{F}_E^{30 \times 3}$ |  |
| CMU_86_03 | 1.34 | 1.38 | 1.40 | 1.30 |  |
|  | (4.92) | (4.80) | (4.79) | (4.35) |  |

model. On the other hand the windowed feature sets $\mathcal{F}_E^{15 \times 3}$, $\mathcal{F}_E^{15 \times 5}$, or $\mathcal{F}_E^{30 \times 3}$ give almost identical results, as do their frame-based counterparts. Also exact nearest-neighbor-searches can be substituted with approximate ones using $\epsilon = 0.5$ without changing the reconstruction results notably.

### 2.5.3 Fast Fat Graphs

We can also come up with a method of substituting the quadratic preprocessing time in the construction of so-called "fat graphs" [SO06]—a method for motion synthesis—with one in $O(n \log n)$ by using kd-tree-based searches. The crucial step in building "fat graphs" is the computation of so-called "base poses", a clustering of motion capture data collections. For a collection of motion data $D = [d_1 \ldots d_n]$, for which a "fat graph" is to be computed, proceed as follows:

1. Search nearest neighbors for each frame $f \in D$ in a fixed radius $r$; the maximum number of neighbors is limited to $k$. This search can be done in $O(kn \log n)$.

2. Find the pose with maximum number of neighbors and use it as "base pose". This step can be done in $O(n)$.

As $k \ll n$ is constant, the complexity of finding the base poses is only $O(n \log n)$ instead of $O(n^2)$, as is the method used in [SO06].

As we have to use a distance measure related to one of our feature sets, the search criterion will be different from the one used in the original construction of

CHAPTER 2. FAST SIMILARITY SEARCHES

"fat graphs". However, in the experiments we performed, the synthesized motions differ only slightly from the ones generated using the original fat graph approach. Moreover, the visual quality of both results is comparable. We refer to the accompanying video for examples.

## 2.6 Including Physics

The properties of a pose can not only be described statically. If we want to describe the kinematic properties of a motion sequence we can either regard a window of frames or consider velocities and accelerations as well.

While the 20 dimensional feature set $\mathcal{F}_{pca}^{pva20}$ described by Arikan et al. [AFO03] can be used in fast kd-tree-based similarity searches, this feature set is strongly biased towards accelerations of human motions, since the observed variance in accelerations is much higher than in velocities or joint positions. Because of that fact this feature set is not well correlated to any of the other feature sets.

Instead we propose to use specific physics-based features, which can be estimated using standard mass distributions for human limbs, e.g., using a population average obtained from [Lev96].

### 2.6.1 Physics-based feature sets

In many motion sequences periods can be found where the body has no contact with the environment. Such phases are known as free flight phases. It is assumed that no external forces, except gravity, have effect on the human body during these phases. For the detection of free flight phases physical properties can be used. Already the acceleration of the center of mass (COM) gives central information about the motion at a single point in time. Its one-dimensional projection onto the direction of gravity can be used to identify ground contact, other contact with the environment or free flight phases.

Another very useful one dimensional physical feature is the projection of the angular momentum onto the direction of gravity, e.g., it very well distinguishes between

## 2.6. INCLUDING PHYSICS

"left turns" and "right turns" in locomotions. The distinction between a left and right turn in a walking motion and the detection of rotational movements is very difficult at a geometric level using kinematic features. Therefore, rotational parts of motions can be better described by dynamic properties. Here rotations around specific axes are of particular interest. Projecting the full body angular momentum onto the gravitational axis allows a distinction of turning movements around the vertical axis, and thus between left and right turns on the floor. By projecting onto a suitable plane, a scalar property is sufficient to distinguish between clockwise and counter clockwise rotations. In a straight walking motion minimal turns to both sides are typical. Typical for a straight walking motion is thus a permanent change in sign of this feature. For a clockwise rotation around the axis of projection the sign is positive, for a counterclockwise rotation it is negative. By regarding the sign different rotations can be differentiated from each other. Thus, this feature is not only well applicable for high-dynamic motions and phases without contact—the settings in which it has been previously used in the context of computer animation [LP02, SP05, ALP06, SH05]—but for many other classes of motions too.

In addition to the detection of rotations around the vertical axis one can choose any arbitrary planes or axes of rotation for the definition of dynamic features. For example, the axes of the whole body motion direction can be used in combination with the whole body velocity. In many cases the rotational part in the direction of the motion is of special interest. Therefore, the projection of the angular momentum along the axis perpendicular to the axis velocity and gravity is useful. This can distinguish a cartwheel or handspring from a normal walking motion, for example.

When computing these features, we scale the velocity and momentum features linearly with the time interval $\Delta t$ under consideration, and acceleration and force features quadratically with $\Delta t^2$. This scaling is a natural one with respect to physical dimensions, and corresponds to a Taylor expansion up to degree two of a non-linear motion function.

In particular, for the experiments in this section we make use of the following feature sets:

$\mathcal{F}_{EP}^{17}$ Similar to $\mathcal{F}_{E}^{15}$, additionally the acceleration of the center of mass in direction of gravity—estimated from standard mass distribution and the angular momentum projected to the direction of gravity are included.

$\mathcal{F}_{EP}^{19}$ Similar to $\mathcal{F}_{E}^{15}$, additionally the acceleration of the center of mass in direction of gravity, and in direction of velocity orthogonal to gravity; angular momentum in direction of gravity and in direction of velocity orthogonal to gravity are included.

## 2.6.2 Experiments and Results

We performed additional experiments for numerical as well as "logical" similarity searches to compare kinematic feature sets and feature sets that include additional physical properties.

**Numerical similarity on a sample database**

For the sake of simplicity only a small sample database containing seven steps of a person walking in a circle to the left, starting with the right foot (frames 1 to 110), a turn (frames 110 to 160), six steps walking in a circle to the right (frames 160 to 270) and stand at place (frames 270 to 300) was used. As query a motion containing two steps walking on a left circle, starting with the right foot was used. As can be seen from the similarity matrices (cf. Figure 2.9), the pose based feature sets exhibit ascending as well as descending diagonal structures, corresponding to similar frames of query and database. Hence such pose-based feature sets are not suitable for separating forward and reverse cycles of motions (e.g., walking and running). Note that the windowed feature sets do not suffer from this issue. Nevertheless, the global motion matching algorithm is able to identify the expected walking motions regardless of the feature set that was used for alignment. Also, as intended the physics-based feature sets (Figure 2.9, lower part) correctly identify frames corresponding to walking in a circle to the left and exclude alignments including also circles to the right. As the structure of the similarity matrices suggests the task of finding warping paths is less constrained for the frame-based feature sets and thus more costly since more potential alignments need to be investigated.

**Numerical and logical similarity**

We performed experiments similar to the ones described in Section 2.5.1 on a large database including physics-based feature sets. Here the use of physical features yields more restricted results, however, falling more closely into the semantic classification given by a human. As can be seen from the accompanying video the semantic classification is debatable—most of the wrongly classified motions are still related (such as "descending" in a walking motion). On the one hand, the effects of using purely geometric features versus the physics-based features is rather transparent for a user and it is desireable to have both variants at hand—for applications in which few but closer matches are required, and for those also looking for broader and even non-physical variations. On the other hand many aspects of the query motion can be captured by regarding the temporal evolution. Thus, simple feature sets like $\mathcal{F}_E^{15}$ give detailed information when used in combination with the lazy neighborhood graph similar to the information included in the stacked feature sets as well as in the physics based feature sets.

## 2.7 Online Method

Based on the lazy neighborhood graph (LNG) an online capable version called "online lazy neighborhood graph" (OLNG) was developed in a later work. It was applied for searching similar motion segments based on accelerometer data by Tautges et al. [TZK⁺11]. Based on the searching results a technique for the reconstruction of human motions from accelerometer data was presented. The main idea of the OLNG is to use a sliding window over the query motion sequence. This allows to reuse the local neighbors and the graph structure already computed for previous frames and only add the neighbors and edges for a current query frame. In addition modified step size conditions allow to skip single frames in the graph structure. Based on these modifications a significant speedup is possible so that the global nearest-neighbor-search can be used in online scenarios.

I refer to Figure 2.10 for an illustrating example, taken from [TZK⁺11]. The motion texturing approach described in Section 4.2 makes use of this extended online version, too.

## 2.8 Conclusion and Future Work

In this work, efficient approaches for local and global motion matching, which are applicable even to huge databases, have been presented. Using these novel techniques we have reduced the time complexity of being quadratic to the size of the motion database $n$ to one of at most $O(n \log n)$ for three very different applications in the realm of data-driven animation. From a practical point of view this means an enhanced applicability of these methods to large databases.

We presume that for other problems something similar can be achieved. In particular, we also consider the adaption of our approaches for local and global motion matching to parametric motion graphs [HG07] and interpolated motion graphs [SH07]. Moreover, the technique described by Chai and Hodgins [CH07] to generate animations from user defined constraints, which uses a global preprocessing on a medium-sized database of human motions seems to be localizable by our technique and thus extendable to huge databases involving very different motions.

It turned out that fast kd-tree-based nearest-neighbor-searches together with viable medium-dimensional feature sets are highly practical even for amounts of motion capture data bigger by two orders of magnitude than has been done with any previously applied technique.

The kd-trees for even the largest motion capture databases currently available still fit into main memory on current standard PCs, and the memory requirements for kd-trees are much lower than the ones required when using locality sensitive hashing for the same data. Nevertheless, our techniques would not scale well if the kd-trees did not fit into the main memory. An adaptation to out-of-core-techniques, e.g., lazy kd-trees [Nar96, HMF07], will become a topic of future research if the available mocap data grow faster than the available main memory.

On the basis of our techniques, data-driven approaches requiring nearest-neighbor-searches on motion data can work efficiently on much larger collections

## 2.8. CONCLUSION AND FUTURE WORK

of motion capture databases than are currently available.

The techniques described in this chapter have been applied in several later works: The Pose searching algorithm has been used in the context of motion synthesis by so called "motion fields" [LWB+10] and the "dynamic motion graphs" Section 4.3 and in the area of cleaning motion capture data [BKZW11b, BKZW11a]. The comparison of different feature sets given in Section 2.4.2 give some basic ideas for a closer evaluation based on a perceptual study [KBAW11].

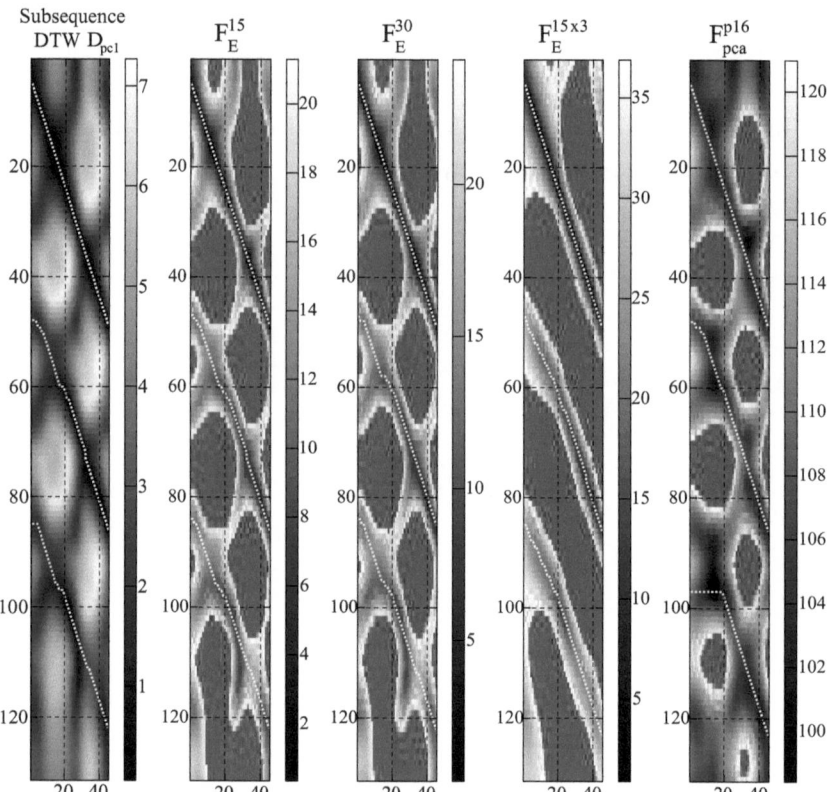

*Figure 2.8: Aligning a query motion segment to similar motions of a small database. The distance matrices implicitly computed by our approach are plotted for four different feature sets. A distance matrix based on $\mathcal{D}_{pcl}$ and warping paths computed by subsequence DTW are shown for comparison. Please note that only frames found during k-nearest-neighbor-search (indicated by shades of grey, the darker the more similar) need to be considered explicitly and that the blue regions do not have to be computed. The red lines represent the recovered warping paths.*

## 2.8. CONCLUSION AND FUTURE WORK

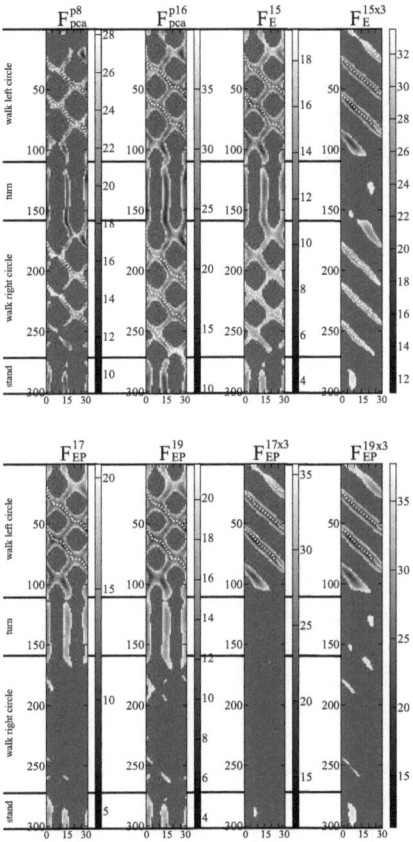

*Figure 2.9: Aligning a query motion segment (walk left circle) to similar motions of a small database. The distance matrices implicitly computed by our approach are plotted for eight different feature sets. Please note that only frames found during k-nearest-neighbor-search (indicated by shades of grey, the darker the more similar) need to be considered explicitly and that the blue regions do not have to be computed. The red lines represent the recovered warping paths. The green annotations describe the motion classes of the small database. The feature sets including physical properties distinguish between walking a left and walking a right circle.*

## CHAPTER 2. FAST SIMILARITY SEARCHES

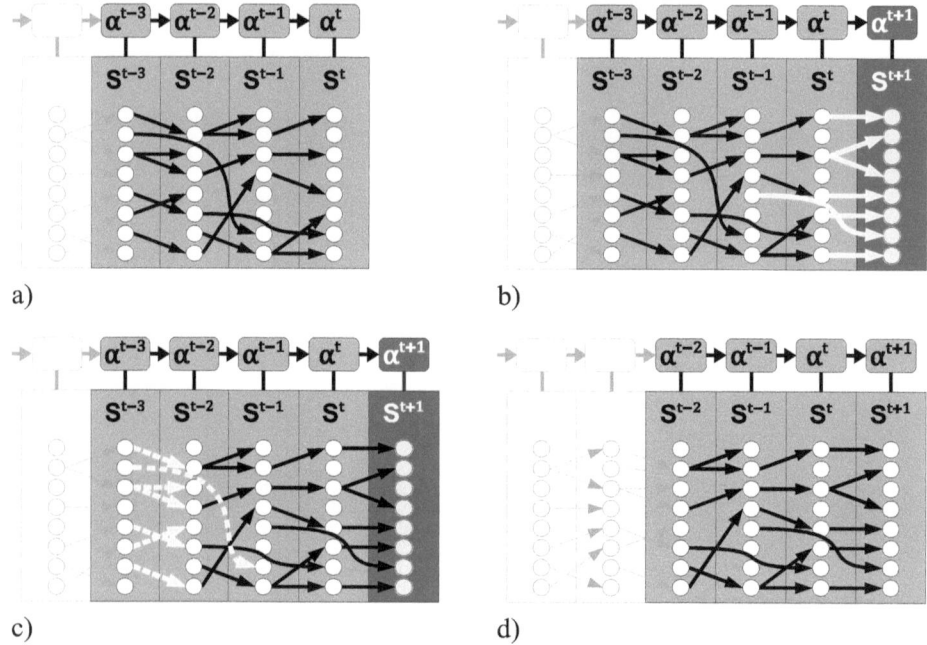

Figure 2.10: Online Lazy Neighborhood Graph (OLNG) with window size $M = 4$ and $K = 8$ nearest neighbors. Each vertical column corresponds to the $K$ nearest neighbors (each neighbor indicated by a circle) of a sensor reading $\alpha^{t-m+1}$, $m \in [1 : M]$. The edges encode temporal coherence between the nearest neighbors. The figure illustrates the implementation of the OLNG [TZK+11]. a) An OLNG is computed to frame $t$ of the query motion. b) A new query frame $t + 1$ is added: The set of nearest neighbors is found by the knn-search. New edges (white) are added according to the given stepsize conditions. c) The neighbors and edges of the first frame are deleted to match the window size. d) OLNG for the frame $t + 1$.

*"Under the bridge downtown is where I drew some blood,
under the bridge downtown I could not get enough,
under the bridge downtown forgot about my love,
under the bridge downtown I gave my life away!"*

Red Hot Chili Peppers – Under the bridge

# 3
# Motion Annotation

Our work is based on various motion representations and retrieval techniques [KTMW08, Mül07, MRC05, MR06]. In this chapter, we extend previous work not only by presenting novel annotation and parametrization procedures but also by introducing a multi-layer annotation framework accounting for different needs in motion analysis and synthesis applications.

In this chapter, we present a multi-layer approach for automatically annotating and parameterizing large unstructured collections of mocap data at different temporal and semantic levels of granularity. Such a multi-layer description, which comprises information on the overall course of a motion as well as on finer motion details, accounts for different needs in computer animation tasks. To be more precise, assume we are given an unknown mocap document. Then the annotation task is to segment the document into logical units and to locally classify and parametrize each segment according to a given set of motion classes. Here, note that the problem of *locally* annotating unknown motion data on the subsegment level is a much harder task than

## CHAPTER 3. MOTION ANNOTATION

*globally* comparing and classifying motion data on the document level.

In our annotation scenario, we assume that each motion class is specified by a set of semantically related example motions which reflect the range of spatio-temporal variations appearing in valid motion realizations. Furthermore, each motion class is partitioned into subclasses, where each subclass represents a specific stylistic aspect. For each motion class, we automatically derive two different types of class representations, which are used in a kind of orthogonal way in the annotation procedure. As a first class representation, we learn a *motion template* (MT) that captures the common as well as the varying aspects of the underlying training motions in an explicit and semantically interpretable matrix representation [MR06, Mül07]. The MT based annotation procedure can be assisted by a key frame-based search algorithm, which not only efficiently narrows the set of candidate motions related to a specific motion class but also improves the annotation quality by eliminating false positive matches [BMS08, MBS09]. As a second class representation, we build up a *motion tensor*, where one mode of the tensor corresponds to the various styles given by the subclasses [KTMW08, KTW07].

**Contributions**

As the key contribution in this chapter, we present a comprehensive multi-layer framework for annotating and parametrizing unknown motion data on different temporal and semantic levels. Based on the concept of motion templates, we make use of an annotation procedure that locally labels a motion document according to a given set of motion classes (Section 3.2.1). The class label can be regarded as a coarse annotation that roughly describes the overall course of the motion. This first step is assisted by a key frame-based search algorithm, which not only efficiently narrows the set of candidate motions related to a specific motion class but also improves the annotation quality by eliminating false positive matches. Based on the concept of motion tensors, we describe a novel analysis-by-synthesis parametrization procedure, which is used to further classify the coarse annotated motion segments according to finer motion subclasses (Section 3.3). To prove the practicability of our annotation and parametrization approach, we describe various experiments conducted on motion documents obtained from the two freely available motion capture databases HDM05 [MRC⁺07] and CMU [Car04]. As our experiments show, the techniques introduced by us are suitable to obtain robust and accurate motion annotations even in the presence of large motion variations. Based on suitable classes, our framework is easily adaptable to specific user needs by simply modifying the motion classes.

## 3.1 Related Work

The use of prerecorded motion capture data to create new realistic motions has become a standard technique in data-driven computer animation [GP00, PB02, AFO03, KG04, CH05, CHP07]. In view of motion synthesis applications, one needs specialized and controlled data sets which are often obtained from manually annotated material. For example, Rose et al. [RCB98] group similar example motions into "verb" classes to synthesize new, user-controlled motions by suitable interpolation techniques. For synthesizing new motions from motion graphs, Kovar et al. [KGP02] allow the use of annotation constraints. However, no techniques are described for the automatic generation of such annotations. Arikan et al. [AFO03] show how to use SVMs to semi-automatically generate annotations, which are then used for motion synthesis. In the last years, various retrieval and classification algorithms have been proposed to automate the annotation process, see, e. g., [WCYL03, KG04, KPZ⁺04, FF05, LZWM05, MRC05, MR06]. Here, the main difficulty arises from the fact that semantically similar motions may reveal significant numerical differences [KG04, MRC05]. Most of the procedures cited above use motion representations that are semantically close to the raw data. Here, problems occur when one has to cope with strong pose deformations within a class of logically related motions. Approaches such as [LZWM05, MRC05] absorb spatial and temporal variations already on the feature level, which then allows for a more robust and efficient motion comparison. Several approaches to classification and recognition of motion patterns are based on hidden Markov models, which are also a flexible tool to capture spatio-temporal variations, see, e. g., [BH00]. Temporal segmentation of motion data can be viewed as another form of anno-

CHAPTER 3. MOTION ANNOTATION

tation, where consecutive, logically related frames are organized into groups, see, e. g., [BSP+04]. Our work is based on various motion representations and retrieval techniques [KTMW08, Mül07, MRC05, MR06]. For a review of this literature, we refer to the subsequent sections. In this chapter, we extend previous work not only by presenting novel annotation and parametrization procedures but also by introducing a multi-layer annotation framework accounting for different needs in motion analysis and synthesis applications.

## 3.2 Annotation via Class Motion Templates

This section gives a short introduction to Motion Templates (MT) introduced by Müller and Röder [MR06, Mül07], the annotation procedure that is supported by the key frame-based searching algorithm by Baak et al. [BMS08, MBS09] and reports on a series of experiments on the coarse annotation level. For a more detailed description we refer to the original works of the authors.

### 3.2.1 Motion Templates

We now summarize the main idea of motion templates and refer to [MR06] for details. As underlying feature representation, we use the concept of relational features that capture semantically meaningful boolean relations between specified points of the kinematic chain underlying the mocap data, see [MRC05]. In the following, we use a set of $f = 40$ relational features, where the first 39 features are defined as in [MR06] and the last feature expresses whether the angular velocity of the root orientation is high or not. Now, given a class $C$ consisting of $\gamma \in \mathbb{N}$ example motions, the goal is to automatically learn a motion class representation that grasps the essence of the class. We start by computing the relational feature vectors for each of the $\gamma$ motions. Denoting the length of a given motion by $K$, we think of the resulting sequence of feature vectors as a *feature matrix* $X \in \{0, 1\}^{f \times K}$.

Next, we compute a semantically meaningful average over the $\gamma$ feature matrices. To cope with temporal variations in the example motions, we use an iterative

## 3.2. ANNOTATION VIA CLASS MOTION TEMPLATES

warping and averaging algorithm [Mül07], which converges to an output matrix $X_C$ referred to as a *motion template* (MT) for the class $C$. The matrix $X_C$ has real-valued entries between zero and one and has a length (number of columns) corresponding to the average length of the training motions. The important observation is that zero/one values in a class MT indicate periods in time (horizontal axis) where certain features (vertical axis) consistently assume the same values zero/one in all training motions, respectively. By contrast, non-zero and non-one values indicate inconsistencies mainly resulting from variations in the training motions. In other words, the zero/one values encode characteristic aspects that are shared by all motions, whereas other values represent the class variations coming from different realizations. Finally, for a given class MT $X_C$, we introduce a *quantized MT* by replacing each entry of $X_C$ that is below a quantization threshold $\delta$ by zero, each entry that is above $1 - \delta$ by one, and all remaining entries by a *wildcard character* $*$ indicating that the corresponding value is left unspecified. In our experiments, we use the threshold $\delta = 0.05$ that has turned out to yield a good trade-off between robustness to motion variations and discriminative power.

### 3.2.2 Annotation procedure

At this point we give a short review of the annotation procedure based on motion templates, that is explained in detail in the original work [MBS09].

**Distance Function**

Given a mocap document $D$ and a specific motion class $C$, a distance function $c^Q(k, \ell)$ that reveals all motion subsegments of $D$ correlating to $C$ can be defined, similar to the original works [MR06] (Section 5.2). The concept of the employed distance function $c^Q(k, \ell)$ only accounts for the consistent entries of $X$ with $X(k)_i \in \{0, 1\}$ and leaves the other entries unconsidered. Based on this local distance measure and a subsequence variant of dynamic time warping (DTW), one obtains a distance function $\Delta_C : [1 : L] \to \mathbb{R} \cup \{\infty\}$ as described in [Mül07] with the following interpretation: a small value $\Delta_C(\ell)$ for some $\ell \in [1 : L]$ indicates the presence of a motion subsegment of $D$ that is similar to the motions in $C$ starting at a suitable frame index $a_\ell < \ell$ and ending at frame index $\ell$.

**Annotation procedure**

The basic idea of the annotation procedure is to locally compare a mocap document with the various class motion templates and then to annotate all frames within a suitable motion segment with the label of the motion class that best explains the segment.

Therefore a modified distance function $\bar{\Delta}_p^\tau : [1 : L] \to \mathbb{R} \cup \{\infty\}$ with respect to a given matching threshold $\tau$ is defined iteratively [MBS09] (Section 4). Here, the idea is that $\bar{\Delta}_p^\tau$ quantitatively describes which frames of the unknown mocap document $D$ closely correlate to motion class $C_p$.

Finally, we minimize the resulting functions over $p \in [1 : P]$ to obtain a single function $\Delta^{\min} : [1 : L] \to \mathbb{R} \cup \{\infty\}$:

$$\Delta^{\min}(\ell) := \min_{p \in [1:P]} \bar{\Delta}_p^\tau(\ell), \quad (3.1)$$

$\ell \in [1 : L]$. Furthermore, we store for each frame the minimizing index $p \in [1 : P]$ yielding a function $\Delta^{\arg} : [1 : L] \to [0 : P]$ defined by:

$$\Delta^{\arg}(\ell) := \operatorname*{argmin}_{p \in [1:P]} \bar{\Delta}_p^\tau(\ell), \quad (3.2)$$

where $\Delta^{\arg}(\ell)$ is set to 0 in the case $\Delta^{\min}(\ell) = \infty$. On principle, the function $\Delta^{\arg}$ yields the annotation of the mocap document $D$ by means of the class labels $p \in [1 : P]$.

**Key frame-based Preselection**

Our annotation procedure may cause a number of false positive annotations. For example, the motion class 'grabDepR', which consists of right hand grabbing and depositing motions, causes a number of confusions with other classes. The reason is that grabbing and depositing motions are rather short motions that possess only few characteristic aspects (basically, the right hand is moving and nothing else happens).

## 3.2. ANNOTATION VIA CLASS MOTION TEMPLATES

*Table 3.1: The 15 motion classes used in our experiments.*

| Class ID | class | description | #(subclasses) |
|---|---|---|---|
| $C_1$ | neutral | stand in a neutral position, hands lowered | 1 |
| $C_2$ | tpose | stand in t-pose, hands horizontally extended | 1 |
| $C_3$ | move | 2 steps (start left or right, walk, jog, shuffle, ...) | 26 |
| $C_4$ | turn | turn around left or right | 2 |
| $C_5$ | sitLieDown | sit down on chair or floor, kneel, lie down on floor | 4 |
| $C_6$ | standUp | stand up from chair or floor | 4 |
| $C_7$ | hopOneLeg | jump with left or right leg | 2 |
| $C_8$ | jump | jump with both feet, jumping jack | 3 |
| $C_9$ | kick | kick to front or side with left or right leg | 4 |
| $C_{10}$ | punch | punch to front or side with left or right hand | 4 |
| $C_{11}$ | rotateArms | rotate both or single arms front or back | 6 |
| $C_{12}$ | throwR | throw an item with right hand, sitting or standing | 4 |
| $C_{13}$ | grabDepR | grab or deposit with right arm high, middle, low | 6 |
| $C_{14}$ | cartwheeel | cartwheel with left or right hand starting | 2 |
| $C_{15}$ | exercise | elbow to knee, skier, squat | 4 |

This leads to a rather unspecific class MT, which reveals small distances to many motion fragments that are actually part of other motion classes.

To cope with this problem, we additionally use a key frame-based preprocessing step that allows to eliminate a large number of false positive annotations. Here, a *key frame query* consists of a sequence of key frames, where each key frame is specified by a feature vector in $\{0, 1, *\}^f$ that describes characteristic relations of a specific pose. A key frame can be thought of as a column of a quantized motion template. Then, the general strategy is to extract all parts from the unknown motion database that exhibit feature vectors matching the key frame feature vectors in the correct order within suitable time bounds. For example, for the class 'grabDepR' one may use two key frames enforcing that both feet do not move while the right hand moves to the front (before grabbing) and is pulled back (after grabbing). In this chapter, we use the key frame-based search algorithm as described in [BMS08].

### 3.2.3 Experiments

For our experiments, we assembled an evaluation dataset consisting of 109 mocap documents having an average length of 40 seconds each. The total length amounts to roughly 74 minutes (133 019 frames at 30 Hz). To illustrate the scalability of our annotation procedure, we used mocap data from two different sources: 60 minutes

## CHAPTER 3. MOTION ANNOTATION

were drawn from the HDM05 database [MRC+07] and 14 minutes from the CMU database [Car04]. We manually annotated all 109 documents on the subsegment level according to the 15 classes described in Table 3.1. Furthermore, we generated a training database consisting of nine example motions for each subclass. These example motions were manually cut out from additional HDM05 documents being disjoint to all evaluation documents. We implemented the annotation algorithms in MATLAB while passing time critical parts to subroutines implemented in C/C++. The experiments were run on an AMD Athlon™ 64 X2 5000+ with 3.5 GB of RAM.

We now describe two performance measures that are used to evaluate our annotation procedure. As a first measure, we consider precision and recall values on the frame level. More precisely, for a given mocap document $D$ of length $L$ we define the sets

$$M(D) := \{(\ell, p) \in [1:L] \times [1:P] \mid \text{frame } \ell \text{ manually annotated by } p\}$$

and

$$A(D) := \{(\ell, p) \in [1:L] \times [1:P] \mid \text{frame } \ell \text{ automatically annotated by } p\}.$$

In other words, the set $M(D)$ describes the manually generated or *relevant* annotations, whereas the set $A(D)$ describes the automatically generated or *retrieved* annotations produced by our procedure. Then, $P_1(D) := \frac{|M(D) \cap A(D)|}{|A(D)|}$ expresses the precision and $R_1(D) = \frac{|M(D) \cap A(D)|}{|M(D)|}$ the recall of our annotation procedure. Furthermore, let $F_1(D) := \frac{2P_1(D)R_1(D)}{P_1(D)+R_1(D)}$ be the resulting F-measure. Intuitively, $P_1(D) = 1$ in the case that all retrieved annotations are among the relevant annotations (no "false positive"), whereas $R_1(D) = 1$ in the case that all relevant annotations have been retrieved. Note that the beginning and ending of a motion of a specific class is often ambiguous. For example, consider a mocap document showing a person who sits down on a chair and remains seated for a long time. Then, it is not clear where exactly to set the end frame when manually annotating the document with respect to the class 'sitDownChair'. Also certain motion transitions from one class to another (e.g., from 'move' to 'turn') can often not be exactly specified. To account for such ambiguities, we use

## 3.2. ANNOTATION VIA CLASS MOTION TEMPLATES

*Table 3.2: Various performance measures for our MT-based annotation procedure.*

|       |            | $P_1$ | $R_1$ | $F_1$ | $P_2$ | $R_2$ | $F_2$ |
|-------|------------|-------|-------|-------|-------|-------|-------|
| total | no keyf.   | 0.48  | 0.79  | 0.59  | 0.57  | 0.91  | 0.70  |
|       | with keyf. | 0.73  | 0.84  | 0.78  | 0.80  | 0.95  | 0.87  |
| HDM   | no keyf.   | 0.49  | 0.80  | 0.61  | 0.61  | 0.91  | 0.73  |
|       | with keyf. | 0.74  | 0.86  | 0.80  | 0.84  | 0.96  | 0.89  |
| CMU   | no keyf.   | 0.41  | 0.75  | 0.53  | 0.39  | 0.90  | 0.54  |
|       | with keyf. | 0.67  | 0.72  | 0.69  | 0.61  | 0.91  | 0.73  |

a second performance measure by considering precision and recall on the segment level. Here, we only check if a manually annotated motion segment with class label $p$ has an overlap with an automatically generated segment with the same class label $p$. We then define the segment-based precision $P_2(D)$, recall $R_2(D)$, and F-measure $F_2(D)$ analogously to the frame-based case.

To compute the performance measures on an entire set of mocap documents, we simply concatenate the various documents to form a single document and apply the above calculation steps.

We computed the various performance measures for the 109 documents of our evaluation datasets using our annotation procedure once without and once with the key frame-based preselection step. The results are shown in Table 3.2. For example, the precision $P_1$ without using key frames is 0.48 and increases significantly to 0.73 when using key frames. At the same time, the recall $R_1$ slightly increases from 0.79 to 0.84. While the increase of the precision is expected, the increase of the recall is somewhat surprising. This is due to the fact that by eliminating false positives, some of the relevant annotations that have previously been "overlayed" by false positive annotations, emerge when using our minimization strategy. This again demonstrates that the key frame-based preselection step eliminates a large number of false positive annotations while not loosing (or even yielding) relevant annotations.

As expected, the segment-based precision and recall values are higher than the frame-based values. For example, using key frames, one has $P_2 = 0.80$ (opposed to $P_1 = 0.73$). In other words, only 20% of the retrieved annotated segments are false positives. For the segment-based recall, one obtains $R_2 = 0.95$ (opposed to $R_1 = 0.84$). Here, only 5% of the relevant annotations are missing. Note that the frame-based performance measures are generally too strict whereas the segment-

# CHAPTER 3. MOTION ANNOTATION

based ones are generally too tolerant. So, in summary, the actual performance of our overall annotation procedure can be described by the two F-measures $F_1 = 0.78$ (being pessimistic) and $F_2 = 0.87$ (being optimistic).

To prove scalability, we evaluated our annotation procedure not only on HDM05, but also on CMU data. Table 3.2 shows the various performance measures for the HDM05 and CMU documents, respectively. Due to significant motion variations in the CMU data, which are not well reflected by HDM05 training material, one has a decline in performance. For example, the F-measure of our overall procedure declines from $F_1 = 0.80$ respective $F_2 = 0.89$ for HDM05 data to $F_1 = 0.69$ respective $F_2 = 0.73$ for CMU data.

In all the above experiments, we used the matching threshold $\tau = 0.13$. Actually, the choice of $\tau$ influences the quality of the overall annotation result. Note that a small value of $\tau$ poses a stronger condition on what to consider similar, thus leading to higher precision and lower recall, while a large value of $\tau$ has the opposite effect. To find a good trade-off of having high precision as well as high recall, we computed the various performance measures for different values of $\tau$.

Our final choice of $\tau = 0.13$ is motivated by the request of having high recall values possibly at the expense of some additional false positive annotations. The false annotations can then be eliminated by more refined annotation procedures on a finer level as described in Section 3.3.

## 3.3 Parametrization via Class Motion Tensors

The previously described MT-based annotation procedure was designed to reliably annotate a given mocap document on a relatively coarse temporal and semantic level. We now introduce a parametrization procedure with the complementary goal to reveal the motion details that were previously disregarded. Here, the motion details to be considered are represented by example motions organized in suitable motion subclasses. As underlying data representation we resort to the concept of motion tensors, which is briefly reviewed in Section 3.3.1. Based on the analysis-by-synthesis paradigm, portions of coarsely annotated motion subsegments are represented as

## 3.3. PARAMETRIZATION VIA CLASS MOTION TENSORS

weighted combinations of the example motions (Section 3.3.2). The descriptive style parameters, which correspond to the subclass labels, are then determined from the weights. Our experiments are described in Section 3.3.3.

### 3.3.1 Motion Tensors

In the parametrization step, we use the concept of motion tensors [KTMW08] to represent a motion class. Generally, a *tensor* is a multidimensional array $\Theta \in \mathbb{R}^{d_1 \times d_2 \times \ldots \times d_N}$ based on $N$ indices, where $N \in \mathbb{N}$ is called the *order* of the tensor. The indices $n \in [1:N]$ are referred to as *modes* and the numbers $d_n$ as dimensions of the modes. Sometimes, we also write $\Theta^{d_1 \times \ldots \times d_N}$ to indicate order and dimensions. The tensor $\Theta$ can be decomposed by an $N$-mode singular value decomposition ($N$-mode SVD) into a product of a *core tensor* $\Phi$ having the same size as $\Theta$ and associated orthonormal matrices $U_n$ of dimension $d_n$, $n \in [1:N]$:

$$\Theta = \Phi \times_1 U_1 \times_2 U_2 \times_3 \ldots \times_N U_N. \tag{3.3}$$

For a definition of the product and further details, we refer to [VBPP05, KTMW08].

In the motion context, we use a tensor of order $N = 5$. The first two modes are referred to as *technical modes* and correspond to the degree of freedom of the underlying skeletal model (DOF mode) and to the length of the motion in frames (frame mode), respectively. The last three modes are referred to as *natural modes* and correspond to different actors performing the motion sequences (actor mode), to different styles occurring in a motion class (style mode), and to different repetitions available for a specific actor and a specific style (repetition mode), respectively. In the following, we are particularly interested in the natural modes, which typically appear in the context of a motion capture session and correspond to semantically meaningful aspects.

We now describe how to build up a *class motion tensor* $\Theta_C = \Theta_C^{d \times f \times a \times s \times r}$ for a specific motion class $C$. Here, $d$ is the dimension of the DOF mode, $f$ of the frame mode, $a$ of the actor mode, $s$ of the style mode, and $r$ of the repetition mode. First, we assume that the class $C$ is partitioned into $s$ subclasses representing the

## CHAPTER 3. MOTION ANNOTATION

various styles or ways to perform a motion belonging to $C$. For example, the class 'sitLieDown' may be partitioned into the $s = 4$ subclasses 'sitDownFloor', 'sitDownChair', 'lieDownFloor', and 'kneelDown'. Each subclass, in turn, is represented by $a \cdot r$ example motions containing $r$ different performances (repetitions) of each of the $a$ different actors. Now, each example motion is modeled as matrix $M \in \mathbb{R}^{d \times f_M}$, where the integer $d \in \mathbb{N}$ refers to the DOFs needed to represent a pose of an underlying skeleton (e. g., encoded by Euler angles or quaternions) and the integer $f_M \in \mathbb{N}$ refers to the number of frames of the respective motion sequence. Before building up a class motion tensor, we first establish temporal correspondence between the various example motions while bringing them to the same reference length $f$. This task can be accomplished by techniques based on dynamic time warping (DTW) using a reference motion consisting of $f$ frames [BW95, KTMW08, Mül07]. The tensor $\Theta_C$ is then defined as the multidimensional array formed by the $a \cdot s \cdot r$ warped example motions of dimension $d \cdot f$.

As indicated by (3.3), a motion tensor $\Theta_C$ can be decomposed into a core tensor $\Phi_C$ and related matrices $U_1, \ldots, U_5$. In this decomposition each matrix $U_n$ corresponds to a specific mode and each row in $U_n$ corresponds to a specific aspect, e.g., a specific actor of the actor mode or a specific style of the style mode. In the following sections, we are only interested in the natural modes and therefore combine the technical modes with the core tensor defining $\Psi_C := \Phi_C \times_1 U_1 \times_2 U_2$. This results in the decomposition

$$\Theta_C = \Psi_C \times_3 U_3 \times_4 U_4 \times_5 U_5 \qquad (3.4)$$

Note that each example motion $M$ contained in $\Theta_C$ is parametrized by three row indices referring to the three matrices $U_3$, $U_4$, and $U_5$, respectively. $M$ can then be recovered simply by multiplying $\Psi_C$ with the corresponding rows of the three matrices. Now, the decomposition (3.4) can be used in an obvious way to synthesize new motion by multiplying $\Theta_C$ with linear combinations of respective matrix rows. More precisely, we express the linear combinations by a list of parameter vectors $\lambda = (\alpha, \beta, \gamma) \in \mathbb{R}^a \times \mathbb{R}^s \times \mathbb{R}^r$ and define

$$M_\lambda := \Psi_C \times_3 \alpha^T U_3 \times_4 \beta^T U_4 \times_5 \gamma^T U_5. \qquad (3.5)$$

## 3.3. PARAMETRIZATION VIA CLASS MOTION TENSORS

Intuitively, the motion $M_\lambda$ is obtained by interpolating (or extrapolating) the example motions using the entries of $\alpha$, $\beta$, and $\gamma$, which can be interpreted according to the structure of the tensor. For example, a large entry $\beta_2$ dominating the other entries in the parameter vector $\beta = (\beta_1, \ldots, \beta_s)$ indicates that the aspect or style expressed by the second subclass dominates the motion $M_\lambda$. This property lies the foundation for our parametrization and annotation procedure.

### 3.3.2 Parametrization Procedure

Now, suppose we are given a motion tensor $\Theta_C$ for the motion class $C$ and a motion segment $M$ annotated by $C$ (e.g., using the annotation procedure described in Section 3.2.1). First, we time-warp $M$ to obtain a motion $M'$ that has a length equal to the dimension $f$ of the frame mode (here, we use an average motion of $\Theta_C$ as reference). The idea is to synthesize a motion $\tilde{M}'$ using $\Theta_C$ that best approximates or explains $M'$. This can be formulated by the following optimization problem:

$$\tilde{M}' := \min_\lambda \left(\mathrm{dist}(M', M_\lambda)\right), \tag{3.6}$$

where the minimization is performed over a suitable subrange of $\mathbb{R}^a \times \mathbb{R}^s \times \mathbb{R}^r$ and $M_\lambda$ is defined as in (3.5). The distance $\mathrm{dist}(M', M_\lambda)$ is measured using the point cloud distance introduced in [KGP02], which has emerged as suitable similarity measure for morphing applications in computer animation. However, in our scenario, the point cloud is taken over the entire motion sequences instead of using local frame windows. Let $\tilde{M}$ be the dewarped motion of $\tilde{M}'$ reversing the above warping step and let $\tilde{\lambda} = (\tilde{\alpha}, \tilde{\beta}, \tilde{\gamma})$ be the minimizing parameter vectors. Then, in the case that $\tilde{M}$ is close to the original motion $M$, the entries of the parameter vector $\tilde{\beta}$ indicate the affinity of $M$ to the various styles represented by the subclass motions.

For the optimization, we use the function lsqnonlin from the MATLAB Optimization Toolbox. This function is an implementation of the *large-scale algorithm*, which is designed for solving nonlinear least-square problems. In the optimization, we constrain the entries of $\lambda = (\alpha, \beta, \gamma)$ to the interval $[-0.2, 1.2]$ to increase the optimization speed and to avoid extreme style extrapolations. Finally, we note that the motion tensor $\Phi$ and the matrices $U_n$ of (3.3) can be substantially reduced by truncating insignificant components. In our implementations, we make use of the reduced model to further speed up our optimization procedure. For details, we refer to [KTMW08, VBPP05].

### 3.3.3 Experiments

Our experiments on motion parametrization are based on the datasets described in Section 3.2.3. For each class $C_p$ of Table 3.1, we construct a class motion tensor $\Theta_p := \Theta_{C_p}$ using nine example motions ($a = 3$ actors, $r = 3$ repetitions) per subclass. The number $s$ of subclasses depends on the respective class and ranges between one and six. (For the class 'move' we actually constructed two separate tensors for motions starting with left and right, respectively. Furthermore, we only used $s = 6$ intermediate subclasses comprising the 13 available subclasses.) For later usage, we synthesize an intermediate motion sequence $M_p$ for each $\Theta_p$.

Now, our overall multi-layer annotation procedure works according to the following steps. In the first step, the unknown motion document $D$ is annotated on the coarse level, see Section 3.2.1. The following steps are conducted for all annotated subsegments. Let $S$ be such a subsegment labeled by $p \in [1 : 15]$. In the second step, we locally compare $S$ with the intermediate motion sequence $M_p$ using a subsequence DTW variant based on the point cloud distance (using local frame windows), see [KGP02]. The local DTW variant allows us to identify subsubsegments in $S$ aligned to $M_p$. (Note that $S$ may contain several such subsubsegments.) In the third step, each identified subsubsegment is time-warped using $M_p$ as reference and parametrized by $\Theta_p$ as described in Section 3.3.2. Let $\lambda = (\alpha, \beta, \gamma)$ be the minimizing parameter vector with $\beta = (\beta_1, \ldots, \beta_s)$ referring to the subclasses (style mode). Then the subsubsegment is labeled by the subclass that corresponds to the maximal entry of $\beta$.

As an illustration, have a look at Fig. 3.1 (a), which indicates a multi-layer annotation result. The upper part indicates the MT-based annotations with respect to the 15 classes of Table 3.1 and the lower part the refined tensor-based annotations

## 3.3. PARAMETRIZATION VIA CLASS MOTION TENSORS

with respect to the subclasses (only relevant subclasses are shown). In the underlying motion, the actor first sits down on the floor, stands up, then sits down on a chair, stands up, kneels down, and finally stands up again (with some beginning, intermediate, and final steps). On the coarse annotation level, the three different 'sitLieDown' subsegments were correctly identified and labeled (red boxes in upper part). From these subsegments, suitable subsubsegments were cut out using the subsequence DTW variant (green boxes in upper part) and further classified according to the four subclasses 'sitDownFloor', 'sitDownChair', 'lieDownFloor', and 'kneelDown'. Also on the finer annotation level, all three occurring 'sitLieDown' variants were annotated correctly (green boxes in lower part). Similarly, the three occurring variants of 'standUp' motions were labeled correctly. However, two of the four labeled 'move' subsegments that were identified by the MT-based annotation are lost on the finer annotation level. Here, due to strong deviations, the two subsegments were rejected in the DTW-based cutting step using a quality threshold.

Similarly, Fig. 3.1 (b) and (c) show the multi-layer annotation results for representative HDM05 and CMU documents, respectively. Looking at (b), one can observe that the motions from the class 'grabDepR' (Table 3.1) were subclassified according to the grabbing and depositing height. Note that some of the coarsely annotated subsegments contain several annotated subsubsegments. Furthermore, note that it is very hard to distinguish grabbing and depositing on the kind of mocap data we had in our experiments (the hands are simply modeled by an end effector). Naturally, there is some confusion between these two subclasses. The examples of Fig. 3.1 (b) and (c) are shown and further discussed in the accompanying video.

For a quantitative evaluation of the tensor-based annotation, we conducted the following experiment: We manually cut out 755 motion clips from HDM05 documents (disjoint to the training clips) and manually annotated them according to the subclasses. Using our tensor-based parametrization, 677 or 89.7% of these segments were labeled with the correct subclass. Now, to evaluate the overall multi-layer annotation procedure, we applied the MT-based annotation, the DTW-based cutting, and the tensor-based annotation to 23 of the mocap documents of our evaluation dataset (Section 3.2.3). Manually inspecting the resulting 319 annotated subsubsegments,

CHAPTER 3. MOTION ANNOTATION

it turned out that 85% of these were labeled with the correct subclass (compared to 80% precision $P_2$ on the coarse annotation level, see Table 3.2)). Here, note that a large number of false positive MT-based annotations is already rejected by the DTW-based cutting step. This is justified by the following overall strategy pursued in our multi-level annotation approach: The MT-based annotation step is designed to give a rough picture of *what* happens in the unkown mocap documents thus aiming at high recall, possibly at the cost of precision. The tensor-based annotation step is designed to give a detailed picture of *how* something happens thus aiming at high precision, possibly at the cost of recall.

## 3.4 Conclusion

In this chapter, we presented a multi-layer framework for annotating motion capture data on different semantic and temporal levels. Using motion templates, we are able to identify logically related motions even in the presence of significant numerical differences. Using motion tensors, we are able to capture finer motion details that are specific for a certain subclass or motion style. Based on our tensor-based motion parametrization procedure, we plan to extend our framework in order to capture even finer motion nuances and actor-specific subtleties.

Finally, in our analysis-by-synthesis approach, we globally optimize over the tensor motions to approximate an unknown motion segment. This typically leads to a dominating coefficient in the parametrization allowing for an accurate annotation (at the cost of approximation accuracy). Here, replacing the global by a local optimization, we will further investigate the delicate tradeoff between annotation and approximation accuracy.

## 3.4. CONCLUSION

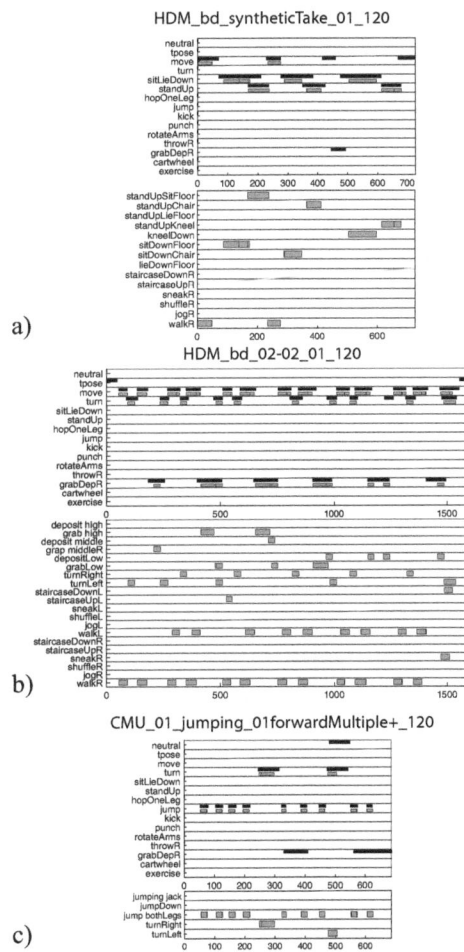

*Figure 3.1:* Representative multi-layer annotation results for three different mocap documents. The upper parts indicate the MT-based annotations with respect to the 15 classes of Table 3.1 and the lower part the refined tensor-based annotations with respect to the subclasses (only relevant subclasses are shown).

*"I hurt myself today to see if I still feel.*
*I focus on the pain, the only thing that's real.*
*The needle tears a hole, the old familiar sting.*
*Try to kill it all away, but I remember everything."*

Jonny Cash – Hurt

# 4

# Motion Synthesis

In this chapter we will present three data-driven methods for the synthesis of human motion data. These methods differ significantly from the necessary semantic pre-classification of the used motion capture data. In Section 4.1 featured multi-linear representations that are based on tensors make use of semantically well-structured and pre-classified motion data. The classification of the motion data can be performed with the annotation technique described in Chapter 3. However, this method also needs pre-classified motion data used for the calculation of the motion templates and the construction of the motion tensors. Since the data have to be pre-classified for these procedure, there would be no advantage in using the fast neighborhood search that is presented in Chapter 2.

In contrast, the procedures for motion synthesis based on dynamic motion graphs (Section 4.3) and texturing of motion data (Section 4.2) make intensive use of these searching techniques. Here no annotation or classification of the underlying motion data is necessary. Thus, we can employ the fast similarity search on unstructured

CHAPTER 4. MOTION SYNTHESIS

motion databases. Both techniques handle the general problem to fill motion data based on incomplete specifications. In our case incomplete motion data can refer to different domains: Motion sequences that are given by using few key frames only, are incomplete in the temporal context. In this case, the dynamic motion graphs (Section 4.3) can be used to generate natural looking animations that satisfy and connect the given key frames. If a motion sequence contains only partially animated poses, e.g., only the lower part of the body is animated, no root motion is given or some poses are damaged by blending, the motion sequence is incomplete in the pose context. In this case, the motion sequence can be completed using the motion texturing process introduced in Section 4.2. The process of motion texturing also can be used as a post-processing of other motion synthesis methods. Thus, the motion segments that were generated using the dynamic motion graph are refined after construction to eliminate artifacts at the transition between different motion segments and to clean-up foot skating.

## 4.1 Multilinear Representation of Motions

In this section, we investigate how a multilinear model can be used to represent human motion data. Based on technical modes (referring to degrees of freedom and number of frames) and natural modes that typically appear in the context of a motion capture session (referring to actor, style, and repetition), the motion data are encoded in the form of a high-order tensor. This tensor is then reduced by using $N$-mode singular value decomposition. Our experiments show that the reduced model approximates the original motion better than previously introduced PCA-based approaches. Furthermore, we discuss how the tensor representation may be used as a valuable tool for the synthesis of new motions.

### 4.1.1 Introduction

Motion capture or mocap systems allow to track and record human motions at high spatial and temporal resolutions. The resulting 3D mocap data are used for motion

## 4.1. MULTILINEAR REPRESENTATION

analysis in fields such as sports sciences, biomechanics, or computer vision, and in particular for motion synthesis in data-driven computer animation. In the last few years, various morphing and blending techniques have been suggested to modify prerecorded motion sequences in order to create new, naturally looking motions, see, for instance, [GP00, Tro02, KGP02, SHP04, KG04, OBHK05, MZF06, CH07, SH07].

In view of motion reuse in synthesis applications, questions concerning data representation, data organization, and data reduction as well as content-based motion analysis and retrieval have become important topics in computer animation. In this context, motion representations based on *linear models* as well as dimensionality reduction techniques via principal component analysis (PCA) have become well-established methods [BSP$^+$04, CH05, FF05, LZWM05, SHP04, GBT04, Tro02, OBHK05]. If no skeleton based representation is used, PCA based techniques on absolute joint positions have been used in the context of compression of motion capture data [Ari06]. Using these linear methods one neglects information of the motion sequences, such as the temporal order of the frames or information about different actors whose motions are included within the database.

In the context of facial animation, Vlasic et al. [VBPP05] have successfully applied *multilinear models* of 3D face meshes that separably parametrizes semantic aspects such as identity, expression, and visemes. The strength of this technique is that additional information can be kept within a multilinear model. For example, classes of semantically related motions can be organized by means of certain modes that naturally correspond to semantic aspects referring to an actor's identity or a particular motion style. Even though multilinear models are a suitable tool for incorporating such aspects into a unified framework, so far only little work has been done to employ these techniques for motion data [Vas02, RCO05, MK06].

In this section, we introduce a multi-linear approach for modeling classes of human motion data. Encoding the motion data as a high-order tensor, we explicitly account for the various modes (e. g., actor, style, repetition) that typically appear in the context of a motion capture session. Using standard reduction techniques based on multi-mode singular value decomposition (SVD), we show that the reduced model

## CHAPTER 4. MOTION SYNTHESIS

approximates the original motion better than previously used PCA-reduced models. Furthermore, we sketch some applications to motion synthesis to demonstrate the usefulness of the multilinear model in the motion context.

The idea of a tensor is to represent an entire class of semantically related motions within a unified framework. Before building up a tensor, one first has to establish temporal correspondence between the various motions while bringing them to the same length. This task can be accomplished by techniques based on dynamic time warping [BW95, GP00, KG03, HPP05]. Most features used in this context are based on spatial or angular coordinates, which are sensitive to data variations that may occur within a motion class. Furthermore, local distance measures such as the 3D point cloud distance as suggested by Kovar and Gleicher [KG03] are computationally expensive. In our approach, we suggest a multiscale warping procedure based on physics-based motion parameters such as center of mass acceleration and angular momentum. These features have a natural interpretation, they are invariant under global transforms, and show a high degree or robustness to spatial motion variation. As a further advantage, physics-based features are still semantically meaningful even on a coarse temporal resolution. This fact allows us to employ a very efficient multiscale algorithm for the warping step. Despite of these advantages, only few works have considered the physics-based layer in the warping context, see [MZF06, SH05].

The remainder of this section is organized as follows. In Section 4.1.2, we introduce the tensor-based motion representation and summarize the data reduction procedure based on singular value decomposition (SVD). The multiscale approach to motion warping using physics-based parameters is then described in Section 4.1.3. We have conducted experiments on systematically recorded motion capture data. As representative examples, we discuss three motion classes including walking, grabbing, and cartwheel motions, see Section 4.1.4. We conclude with Section 4.1.5, where we indicate future research directions. In particular, we discuss possible strategies for the automatic generation of suitable motion classes from a scattered set of motion data, which can then be used in our tensor representation.

## 4.1.2 Multilinear Algebra

Our tensor representation is based on multilinear algebra, which is a natural extension of linear algebra. A *tensor* $\Delta$ of *order* $N \in \mathbb{N}$ and type $(d_1, d_2, \ldots, d_N) \in \mathbb{N}^N$ over the real number $\mathbb{R}$ is defined to be an element in $\mathbb{R}^{d_1 \times d_2 \times \ldots \times d_N}$. The number $d := d_1 \cdot d_2 \cdot \ldots \cdot d_N$ is referred to as the *total dimension* of $\Delta$. Intuitively, the tensor $\Delta$ represents $d$ real numbers in a multidimensional array based on $N$ indices. These indices are also referred to as the *modes* of the tensor $\Delta$. As an example, a vector $v \in \mathbb{R}^d$ is a tensor of order $N = 1$ having only one mode. Similarly, a matrix $M \in \mathbb{R}^{d_1 \times d_2}$ is a tensor of order $N = 2$ having two modes which correspond to the columns and rows. A more detailed description of multilinear algebra is given in [VBPP05].

**Tensor construction**

In our context, we deal with 3D human motion data as recorded by motion capture systems. A (sampled) motion sequence can be modeled as a matrix $M \in \mathbb{R}^{n \times f}$, where the integer $n \in \mathbb{N}$ refers to the degrees of freedom (DOFs) needed to represent a pose of an underlying skeleton (e. g., encoded by Euler angles or quaternions) and the integer $f \in \mathbb{N}$ refers to the number of frames (poses) of the motion sequence. In other words, the $i$th colum of $M$, in the following also denoted by $M(i)$, contains the DOFs of the $i$th pose, $1 \leq i \leq f$. In the following examples, we will work either with an Euler angle representation of a human pose having $n = 62$ DOFs or with a quaternion representation having $n = 119$ DOFs (with $n = 4 \cdot m + 3$ where $m = 29$ is the number of quaternions representing the various joint orientations). In both representations 3 DOFs are used to describe the global 3D position of the root node of the skeleton.

We now describe how to construct a tensor from a given class of semantically related motion sequences. After a warping step, as will be explained in Section 4.1.3, all motion sequences are assumed to have the same number of frames. We will introduce two types of modes referred to as *technical modes* and *natural modes*. We consider two technical modes that correspond to the degrees of freedom and number of frames, respectively:

- **Frame mode**: This mode refers to the number of frames a motion sequence is composed of. The dimension of the frame mode is denoted by $f$.

- **DOF mode**: This mode refers to the degrees of freedom, which depends on the respective representation of the motion data. The dimension of the DOF mode is denoted by $n$.

Sometimes the two technical modes are combined to form a single mode, which is referred to as *data mode*:

- **Data mode**: This mode refers to an entire motion sequence, where all motion parameters are stacked into a single vector. For a motion sequence $M \in \mathbb{R}^{n \times f}$, the dimension of the data mode is $f \cdot n$.

Additionally, we introduce natural modes that typically appear in the context of a motion capture session:

- **Actor mode:** This mode corresponds to the different actors performing the motion sequences. The dimension of the actor mode (number of actors) is denoted by $a$.

- **Style Mode:** This mode corresponds to the different styles occurring in the considered motion class. The meaning of style differs for the various motion classes. The dimension of the style mode (number of styles) is denoted by $s$.

- **Repetition mode:** This mode corresponds to the different repetitions or interpretations, which are available for a specific actor and a specific style. The dimension of the repetition mode (number of repetitions) is denoted by $r$.

The natural modes correspond to semantically meaningful aspects that refer to the entire motion sequence. These aspects are often given by some rough textual description or instruction. The meaning of the modes may depend on the respective motion class. Furthermore, depending on the availability of motion data and suitable metadata, the various modes may be combined or even further subdivided.

## 4.1. MULTILINEAR REPRESENTATION

For example, the style mode may refer to emotional aspects (e. g., furious walking, cheerful walking), motion speed (e. g., fast walking, slow walking), motion direction (e. g., walking straight, walking to the left, walking to the right), or other stylistic aspects (e. g., limping, tiptoeing, marching). Further examples will be discussed in Section 4.1.4. Finally, we note that in [MK06] the authors focus on correlations with respect to joints and time only, which, in our terminology, refer to the technical modes. Furthermore, in [Vas02], the author discusses only a restricted scenario considering leg movements in walking motions.

### $N$-mode SVD

In our experiments, we constructed several data tensors with different numbers of modes from the data base described in Section 4.1.4. The tensor with the smallest number of modes was created by using the three natural modes (Actors, Style, and Repetition) and the data mode. With this arrangement we obtain a tensor in the size of $f \cdot n \times a \times s \times r$. It is also possible to use the Frame and the DOF mode, instead of the data mode, to arrange the same motion sequences within the tensor. The natural modes are not changed when using this strategy. Therefore a tensor of this type has a size of $f \times n \times a \times s \times r$.

Similar to [VBPP05], a data tensor $\Delta$ can be transformed by an $N$-mode singular value decomposition ($N$-mode SVD). Recall that $\Delta$ is an element in $\mathbb{R}^{d_1 \times d_2 \times ... \times d_N}$. The result of the decomposition is a *core tensor* $\Phi$ of the same type and associated orthonormal matrices $U_1, U_2, \ldots, U_N$. The matrices $U_k$ are elements in $\mathbb{R}^{d_k \times d_k}$ where $k \in \{1, 2, \ldots, N\}$. The tensor decomposition in our experiments was done by using the N-way Toolbox [BA00]. Mathematically this decomposition can be expressed in the following way:

$$\Delta = \Phi \times_1 U_1 \times_2 U_2 \times_3 \ldots \times_N U_N. \tag{4.1}$$

This product is defined recursively, where the mode-$k$-multiplication $\times_k$ with $U_k$ replaces each mode-$k$-vector $v$ of $\Phi \times_1 U_1 \times_2 U_2 \times_3 \ldots \times_{k-1} U_{k-1}$ for $k > 1$ (and $\Phi$ for $k = 1$) by the vector $U_k v$.

One important property of $\Phi$ is that the elements are sorted in a way that the

## CHAPTER 4. MOTION SYNTHESIS

variance decreases from the first to the last element in each mode [VBPP05]. A reduced model $\Phi'$ can be obtained by truncation of insignificant components of $\Phi$ and of the matrices $U_k$, respectively. In the special case of a 2-mode tensor this procedure is equivalent to principal component analysis (PCA) [Vas02].

**Motion Reconstruction**

Once we have obtained the reduced model $\Phi'$ and its associated matrices $U'_k$, we are able to reconstruct an approximation of any original motion sequence. This is done by first mode-multiplying the core tensor $\Phi'$ with all matrices $U'_k$, belonging to a technical mode. In a second step the resulting tensor is mode-multiplied with one row of all matrices belonging to a natural mode. Furthermore, with this model at hand, we can generate an arbitrary interpolation of original motions by using linear combinations of rows of the matrices $U'_k$ with respect to the natural modes.

### 4.1.3 Motion Warping

During the last few years, several methods for motion alignment have been proposed which rely on some variant of dynamic time warping (DTW), see, e.g., [BW95, GP00, KG03, MR06]. The alignment or warping result depends on many parameters including the motion features as well as the local cost measure used to compare the features. In this section, we sketch an efficient warping procedure using physics-based motion features (Section 4.1.3) and applying an iterative multiscale DTW algorithm (Section 4.1.3).

**Physics-based Features**

In our approach, we use physics-based motion features to compare different motion sequences. Physics-based motion features are invariant under global transforms and show a high degree of robustness to spatial variations, which are often present in semantically related motions that belong to the same motion class. Furthermore, our features are still semantically meaningful even on a coarse temporal resolution, which allows us to employ them in our multiscale DTW approach.

## 4.1. MULTILINEAR REPRESENTATION

In our experiments, we used two different types of motion features: the center of mass (COM) acceleration and angular momenta for all skeletal segments. The 3D position of the COM is calculated for all segments of the skeleton by using the anthropometric tables described in [RW03]. From these positions and the mass of the segments one can calculate the COM position of the whole body by summing up the products of the 3D centers of mass of each segment and their corresponding mass and dividing this vector afterwards by the mass of the whole body. The second derivative of the resulting 3D positional data stream is the COM acceleration. Our second feature, the angular momentum, is computed for each segment describing its rotational properties. More precisely the angular momentum of how the segment's rotation would continue if no external torque acts on it. It is calculated by the cross product between the vector from the point the segment rotates around to the segment's COM and the vector expressing the linear momentum.

Physics-based features provide a lot of information about the underlying motion sequence. For example, considering the COM acceleration it is easy to detect flight phases. More precisely, in case the body has no ground contact, the COM acceleration is equivalent to the acceleration of gravity:

$$a_{\text{COM}} \approx a_{\text{earth}} = \begin{pmatrix} 0.0 \\ -9.81 \\ 0.0 \end{pmatrix} \quad (4.2)$$

This situation is illustrated by Figure 4.1, which shows the COM acceleration for a dancing motion. Note that there are three flight phases, which are revealed by the vertical component ($y$-axis) of the COM acceleration. Further examples are discussed in Section 4.1.3.

**Multiscale Dynamic Time Warping**

Dynamic time warping (DTW) is a well-known technique to find an optimal alignment (encoded by a so-called warping path) between two given sequences. Based on the alignment, the sequences can be warped in a non-linear fashion to match

CHAPTER 4. MOTION SYNTHESIS

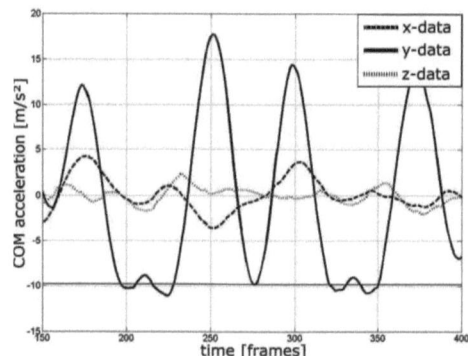

*Figure 4.1: COM acceleration for a dancing motion containing three different jumps. The acceleration is spliced into its x (dotted), y (solid) and z (dashed) component, where the y component refers to the vertical direction. Note that the y component reveals two long flight phases (frames 190 to 220 and frames 320 to 350, respectively) and one short flight phase (around frame 275).*

each other. In our context, each motion sequence is converted into a sequence of physics-based motion features at a temporal resolution of 120 Hz. We denote by $V := (v_1, v_2, \ldots, v_n)$ and $W := (w_1, w_2, \ldots, w_m)$ the feature sequences of the two motions to be aligned. Since one of the motions might be slower than the other, $n$ and $m$ do not have to be equal.

In a second step, one computes an $n \times m$ cost matrix $C$ with respect to some local cost measure $c$, which is used to compare two feature vectors. In our case, we use a simple cost measure, which is based on the inner product:

$$c(v, w) := 1 - \frac{\langle v|w\rangle}{|v|_2 |w|_2} \quad (4.3)$$

for two non-zero feature vectors $v$ and $w$ (otherwise $c(v, w)$ is set to zero). Note that $c(v, w)$ is zero in case $v$ and $w$ coincide and assumes values in the real interval $[0, 1] \subset \mathbb{R}$. Then, the cost matrix $C$ with respect to the sequences $V$ and $W$ is defined by

$$C(i, j) := c(v_i, w_j) \quad (4.4)$$

## 4.1. MULTILINEAR REPRESENTATION

for $1 \leq i \leq n$ and $1 \leq j \leq m$. Figure 4.2 shows such cost matrices with respect to different features.

Finally, an optimal alignment is determined from the cost matrix $C$ via dynamic programming. Such an alignment is represented by a so-called (cost-minimizing) *warping path*, which, under certain constraints, optimally allocates the frame indices of the first motion with the frame indices of the second motion. In Figure 4.2, such optimal warping paths are indicated in red. Note that the information given by an optimal warping path can be used to time-warp the second motion (by suitably omitting or replicating frames) to match the first motion. Further details and references on DTW may be found in [ZM06].

Note that the time and memory complexity of the DTW algorithm is quadratic in the number of frames of the motions to be aligned. To speed up the process, we employ an iterative multiscale DTW algorithm as described in [ZM06]. Here, the idea is to proceed iteratively using multiple resolution levels going from coarse to fine. In each step, the warping path computed at a coarse resolution level is projected to the next higher level, where the projected path is refined to yield a warping path at the higher level. To obtain features at the coarse levels, we use simple windowing and averaging procedures. In this context, the physics-based features have turned out to yield semantically meaningful features even at a low temporal resolution. In our implementation, we used six different resolution levels starting with a feature resolution of 4 Hz at the lowest level. The overall speed-up of this approach (in comparison to classical DTW) depends on the length of the motion sequences. For example, the speed-up amounts to a factor of roughly 10 for motions having 300 frames and a factor of roughly 100 for motions having 3000 frames.

**Examples**

Figure 4.2 shows two cost matrices, where we compared two walking motions both consisting of 6 steps forward. In dark areas the compared poses are similar with respect to the given features, whereas in lighter areas the poses are dissimilar. The red line is the optimal warping path found by the DTW algorithm. The cost matrix on the left side is based only on the COM acceleration of the entire body. Using this

CHAPTER 4. MOTION SYNTHESIS

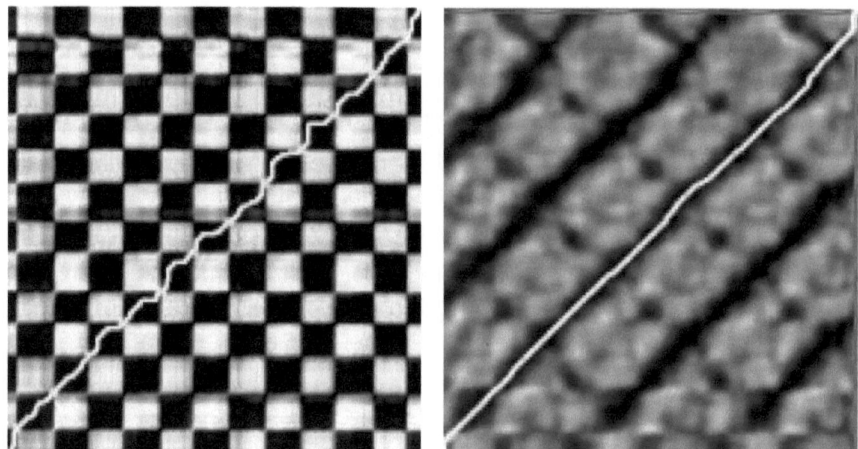

Figure 4.2: *DTW cost matrices calculated on the whole body COM acceleration (left) as well as on the basis of the COM acceleration and the angular momenta of the hands and feet (right). The cost-minimizing warping paths are drawn in red.*

single feature, the checkerboard-like pattern indicates that one cannot differentiate between steps that were done with the left or the right foot. Adding the features that measure the angular momenta of the feet, the result visibly improves. The resulting cost matrix is shown on the right hand side of Figure 4.2. The five dark diagonals indicate that in this case only the steps made with the same foot are regarded as similar.

Depending on the motions to be time-warped, one can select specific features. For walking motions, the movement of the legs contains the most important information in case the steps are to be synchronized. For time-warping grabbing motions as used in our experiments, aspects concerning the right hand were most important as the motions were performed by this hand. For our cartwheel motions, good correspondences were achieved when using features that concern the two hands and the two feet. For an example of warped walking motions, we refer to the accompanying video.

4.1. MULTILINEAR REPRESENTATION

## 4.1.4 Experimental Results

**Data Base**

For our experiments, we systematically recorded several hours of motion capture data containing a number of well-specified motion sequences, which were executed several times and performed by five different actors. The five actors all have been healthy young adult male persons. Using these data, we built up a database consisting of roughly 210 minutes of motion data. Then we manually cut out suitable motion clips and arranged them into 64 different classes and styles. Each motion class contains 10 to 50 different realizations of the same type of motion, covering a broad spectrum of semantically meaningful variations. The resulting *motion class database* contains 1,457 motion clips of a total length corresponding to roughly 50 minutes of motion data [MRC$^+$07]. For our experiments, we considered three motion classes. The first class contains walking motions executed in the following styles:

- Walk four steps in a straight line.

- Walk four steps in a half circle to the left side.

- Walk four steps in a half circle to the right side.

- Walk four steps in place.

All motions within each of these styles had to start with the right foot and were aligned over time to the length of the first motion of actor one.

The second class of motions we considered in our experiments consists of various grabbing motions, where the actor had to pick an object with the right hand from a storage rack. In this example the style mode corresponds to three different heights (low, middle, and high) where the object was located in the rack.

The third motion class consists of various cartwheels. Cartwheel motions were just available for four different actors and for one style. All cartwheels within the class start with the left foot and the left hand.

# CHAPTER 4. MOTION SYNTHESIS

**Motion Preprocessing**

For all motion classes described in the previous section, we constructed data tensors with motion representations based on Euler angles and based on quaternions. Initially some preprocessing was required, consisting mainly of the following steps. All motions were

1. filtered in the quaternion domain with a smoothing filter described as in [LS02],

2. time-warped using physics-based features,

3. normalized by moving the root nodes to the origin and by orienting the root nodes to the same direction,

4. finally sampled down to a frame-rate of 30 Hz.

**Truncation Experiments**

In this section, we discuss various truncation experiments for our three representative example motion classes. In these experiments, we systematically truncated a growing number of components of the core-tensors, then reconstructed the motions, and compared them with the original motions.

Based on the walking motions (using quaternions to represent the orientations), we constructed two data tensors. The first tensor $\Delta_{\text{Walk}}^{f \cdot n \times a \times s \times r}$ was constructed by using the data mode as technical mode. This is indicated by the upper index, which shows the dimension of the tensor. The motions were time-warped and sampled down to a length of 60 frames. The resulting size of $\Delta_{\text{Walk}}^{f \cdot n \times a \times s \times r}$ is $7140 \times 5 \times 4 \times 3$. Using the frame mode and DOF mode, we obtained a second tensor $\Delta_{\text{Walk}}^{f \times n \cdot a \times s \times r}$ of size $60 \times 119 \times 5 \times 4 \times 3$. Table 4.1 shows the results of our truncation experiments. The first column shows the size of the core tensors $\Phi'_{\text{Walk}}$ after truncation, where the truncated modes are colored in red. The second column shows the number of entries of the core tensors, and the third one shows its size in percent compared to $\Delta_{\text{Walk}}$. In the fourth column, the total usage of memory is shown. Note that the total memory

## 4.1. MULTILINEAR REPRESENTATION

requirements may be higher than for the original data, since besides the core tensor $\Phi'$ one also has to store the matrices $U'_k$. The memory requirements are particularly high in case one mode has a high dimension. The last two columns give the results of the reconstruction. $E_{\text{total}}$ is an error measurement which is defined as the sum over the reconstruction error $E_{\text{mot}}$ over all motions:

$$E_{\text{total}} = \frac{1}{a \cdot s \cdot r} \cdot \sum_a \sum_s \sum_r E_{\text{mot}} \qquad (4.5)$$

The reconstruction error $E_{\text{mot}}$ of a motion is defined as normalized sum over all frames and over all joints:

$$E_{\text{mot}} = \frac{1}{f \cdot m} \cdot \sum_{i=1}^{f} \sum_{l=1}^{m} (\arccos(\langle q_{i,l}^{\text{org}} | q_{i,l}^{\text{rec}} \rangle) \cdot 2) \cdot \frac{180}{\pi}, \qquad (4.6)$$

where $f$ denotes the number of frames and $m$ the number of quaternions. Here, for each joint, the original and reconstructed quaternions $q^{\text{org}}$ and $q^{\text{rec}}$ are compared by means of their included angle. We performed a visual rating for some of the reconstructed motions in order to obtain an idea of the quality of our error measurement. Here, a reconstructed motion was classified as good (or better) in case one could hardly differentiate it from the original motion when both of the motions were put on top of each other. The results of our ratings are given in the last column.

If the data mode is split up into the Frame and DOF mode, as in $\Delta_{\text{Walk}}^{f \times n \times a \times s \times r}$, one can truncate the two modes separately. The results are shown in the lower part of Table 4.1 and Figure 4.3. For example, reducing the DOF mode from 60 to 26, the error $E_{\text{total}}$ is still less than one degree. A similar result is obtained by reducing the frame mode down to a size of 20. This shows that there is a high redundancy in the data with respect to the technical modes.

We also conducted experiments where we reduced the dimensions of the natural modes. As the experiments suggest, the dimensions of the natural modes seem to be more important than the ones of the technical modes. The smallest errors (when truncating natural modes) resulted by truncating the repetition mode. This is not surprising since the actors were asked to perform the same motion several times in

# CHAPTER 4. MOTION SYNTHESIS

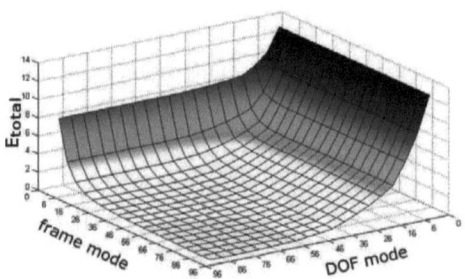

Figure 4.3: Reconstruction error $E_{total}$ for truncated frame and DOF mode.

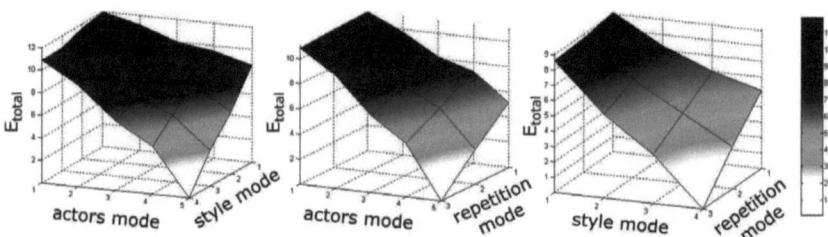

Figure 4.4: Error $E_{total}$ of reconstructed motions where two natural modes were truncated. Actor and style mode are truncated (left). Actor and repetition mode are truncated (middle). Style and repetition mode are truncated (right).

the same fashion. Note that different interpretations by one and the same actor reveal a smaller variance than motions performed by different actors or motions performed in different styles. Some results of our experiments are illustrated by Figure 4.4. The displacement grows with the size of truncated values from style- and personal mode.

For building the data tensors $\Delta_{\text{Grab}}^{f \cdot n \times a \times s \times r}$ and $\Delta_{\text{Grab}}^{f \times n \times a \times s \times r}$, all motions were warped to the length of one reference motion. $\Delta_{\text{Grab}}^{f \cdot n \times a \times s \times r}$ has a size of $8449 \times 5 \times 3 \times 3$, while $\Delta_{\text{Grab}}^{f \times n \times a \times s \times r}$ has a size of $71 \times 119 \times 5 \times 3 \times 3$. The exact values for truncating the data mode and the DOF mode can be found in Table 4.2.

In our third example, we consider a motion class consisting of cartwheel motions. The core tensor $\Delta_{\text{Cart}}^{f \cdot n \times a \times s \times r}$ has a size of $7497 \times 4 \times 1 \times 3$. Here, all motions could be reconstructed without any visible error for a size of no more than 12 dimensions for the data mode. Further results are shown in Table 4.3.

The number of necessary components of the data mode varied a lot in the different

## 4.1. MULTILINEAR REPRESENTATION

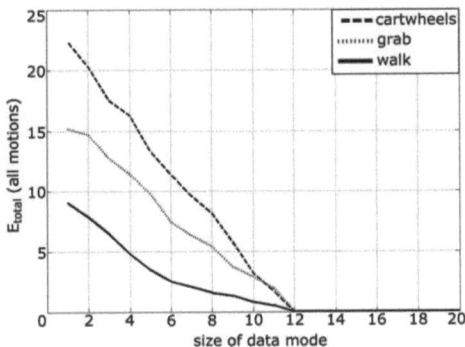

*Figure 4.5:* Reconstruction error $E_{total}$ for walking (solid), grabbing (dotted) and cartwheel (dashed) motions, depending on the size of the data mode of the core tensor.

motion classes. One would expect that a cartwheel motion is more complex than a grabbing or walking motion. The results of previous experiments do not support this prospect. But the results of these truncation experiments are not comparable as they depend on all dimensions of the constructed tensors. To get comparable results for the three motion classes, we constructed a tensor including three motions from three actors for each motion class. The style mode is limited to a size of one, since we have no different styles for cartwheel motions. Therefore the resulting tensors have a size of $f \cdot n \times 3 \times 3 \times 1$. When truncating the data mode of these tensors, one gets the result that is shown in Figure 4.5. All motions are reconstructed perfectly until the size of the data mode gets smaller than 12. At this size the core tensor $\Phi'$ and the matrices $U_k$ have as many entries as the original data tensor $\Delta$. Then the error $E_{total}$ grows different for the three motion classes. The least error is observed for the walking motions (solid). This could be expected for a cyclic motion that contains a lot of redundant frames. The used grabbing motions (dotted) are more complex. The reason may be that the motion sequences differ since some sequences include a step to the storage rack while others do not. The cartwheel motions (dashed) are the most complex class in this experiment, as we expected.

CHAPTER 4. MOTION SYNTHESIS

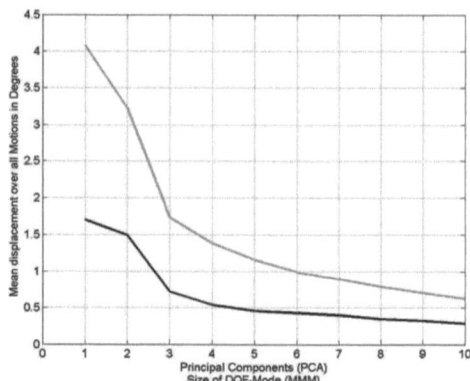

Figure 4.6: *Mean error of reconstructed motions with reconstructions based on our model (black) and based on a PCA (gray). The result is shown for walking motions.*

**Comparison with PCA**

To compare our multilinear model with linear models, as they are used for principal component analysis (PCA), we constructed two tensors for our model and two matrices for the PCA. The first tensor and the first matrix were filled with walking motions, the second tensor and the second matrix were filled with grabbing motions. The orientations were represented by Euler angles. The resulting tensors had a size of $81 \times 62 \times 3 \times 3 \times 3$ (walking) and $64 \times 62 \times 3 \times 3 \times 3$ (grabbing), respectively.

After some data reduction steps, we compared the reconstructed motions with the original motions by measuring the differences between all orientations of the original and the reconstructed motions. Averaging over all motions and differences, we obtained a mean error as is also used in [SHP04] (we used this measure to keep the results comparable to the literature). Figures 4.6 and 4.7 show a comparison of the mean errors in the reconstructed motions for the walking (left) and grabbing (right) examples. The mean errors depend on the size of the DOF mode and the number of principal components, respectively. Note that the errors for motions reconstructed from the multi-mode-model are smaller than the errors from the motions reconstructed from principal components. For example, a walking motion can be reconstructed with a mean error of less than one degree (in the average) from a core

## 4.1. MULTILINEAR REPRESENTATION

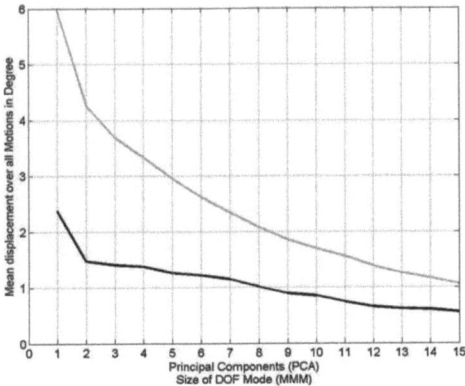

*Figure 4.7: Mean error of reconstructed motions with reconstructions based on our model (black) and based on a PCA (gray). The result is shown for grabbing motions.*

tensor when the DOF mode is truncated to just three components (see left part of Figures 4.6 and 4.7). Therefore, in cases where a motion should be approximated by rather few components the reduction based on the multilinear model may be considerably better than the one achieved by PCA.

**Motion Synthesis**

As described in Section 4.1.2, it is possible to synthesize motions with our multilinear model. For every mode $k$ there is an appropriate matrix $U_k$, where every row $u_{k,j}$ with $j \in \{1, 2, \ldots, d_k\}$ represents one of the dimensions of mode $k$. Therefore an inter- or extrapolation between the $d_k$ dimensions, e.g., between the styles, actors and repetitions, can be done by inter- or extrapolation between any row of $U_k$ before they are multiplied with the core tensor $\Phi$ to synthesize a motion. To prevent our results from artifacts such as turns and unexpected flips resulting from a representation based on Euler angles we used our quaternion based representation to synthesize motions.

For the following walking example, we constructed a motion that was interpolated between two different styles. The first style was walking four steps straight forward and the second one was walking four steps on a left circle. We made a linear

CHAPTER 4. MOTION SYNTHESIS

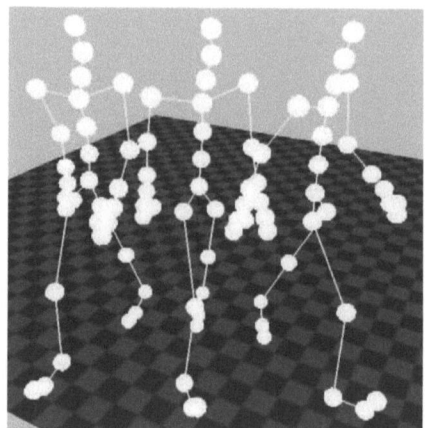

*Figure 4.8: Screenshot from the original motions of the styles walking forward (left) and walking a left circle (right), the synthetic motion (middle) is produced by a linear combination of these styles.*

interpolation by multiplying the corresponding rows with the factor 0.5. The result is a four step walking motion that describes a left round with a larger radius. One sample frame of this experiment can be seen in Figure 4.8. Another synthetic motion was made by an interpolation of grabbing styles. We synthesized a motion by an interpolation of the styles grabbing low and grabbing high. The result is a motion that grabs in the middle. One sample frame of this synthetic motion is shown in Figure 4.9.

With this technique we are able to make interpolation between all modes simultaneously. One example is a walking motion that is an interpolation between the style and actors mode. One snapshot taken from the accompanying animation video of this example is given in Figure 4.9.

**Computation Times**

In Table 4.4 the computation times of our MATLAB implementations of the $N$-mode SVD and PCA are given (on an 1.66 GHz Intel Core2 CPU T5500). For the decomposition of a data tensor $\Delta_{\text{Walk}}^{f \times n \times a \times s \times r}$ consisting of $95 \times 119 \times 4 \times 3 \times 2 = 273600$

## 4.1. MULTILINEAR REPRESENTATION

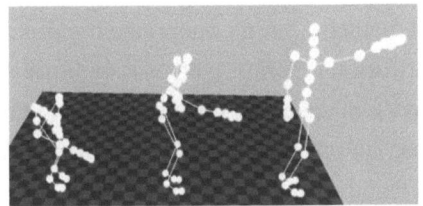 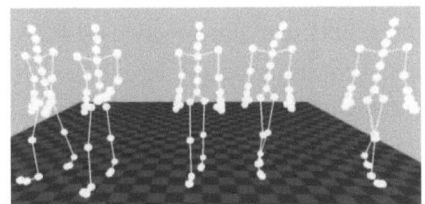

*Figure 4.9:* **Left:** *Screenshot from the original motions of the styles grabbing low (left) and grabbing high (right), the synthetic motion (middle) is produced by a linear combination of these styles.* **Right:** *Screenshot from four original walking motions and one synthetic motion, that is a result of combining two, the personal and the style mode. The original motions of the first actor are on the left side, the original motions of the second actor are on the right side and the synthetic example can be seen in the middle.*

entries, the $N$-mode SVD needs 5.675 seconds, while the PCA needs 0.636 seconds for a matrix of comparable size having $119 \times 2280 = 273\,600$ entries. As Table 4.4 shows, the computing time for the SVD increases with the dimension of the tensor, while the computation time for the PCA is nearly constant.

The SVD decomposition can be seen as a preprocessing step, where all further calculations can be done on the core tensor and the corresponding matrices. The reconstruction of a motion from the tensor $\Phi_{\text{Walk}}^{f \times n \times a \times s \times r}$ and the matrices $U_k$ can be performed at interactive frame rates—even in our MATLAB implementation the reconstruction only requires 0.172 seconds. As a combination of motions of different modes is just a reconstruction with modified weights, the creation of synthetic motions is also possible with a similar computational cost.

### 4.1.5 Conclusion and Future Work

In this Section, we have shown how multilinear models can be used for analyzing and processing human motion data. The representation is based on explicitly using various modes that correspond to technical as well as semantic aspects of some given motion class. Encoding the data as high-order tensors allows for reducing the model with respect to any combination of modes, which often yields better approxima-

## CHAPTER 4. MOTION SYNTHESIS

tion results than previously used PCA-based methods. Furthermore, the multilinear model constitutes a unified and flexible framework for motion synthesis applications, which allows for controlling each motion aspect independently in the morphing process. As a further contribution, we described an efficient multiscale approach for motion warping using physics-based motion features.

Multilinear motion representations constitute an interesting alternative and additional tool in practically all situations in which current PCA-based methods are used. We expect that our multi-modal model is helpful in the context of reconstructing motions from low-dimensional control signals, see, e. g., [CH05]. Currently, we also investigate how one can improve auditory representations of motions as described in [RM05, EMWZ05] by using strongly reduced motion representations.

In order to construct a high-order tensor for a given motion class, one needs a sufficient number of example motions for each mode to be considered in the model. In practice, this is often problematic, since one may only have sparsely given data for the different modes. In such situations, one may employ similar techniques as have been employed in the context of face transfer, see [VBPP05]. Another important research problem concerns the automatic extraction of suitable example motions from a large database, which consists of unknown and unorganized motion material. For the future, we plan to employ efficient content-based motion retrieval strategies as described, e. g., in [KG04, MRC05, MR06] to support the automatic generation of multimodal data tensors for motion classes that have a sufficient number of instances in the unstructured dataset. From these techniques a motion reconstruction based on accelerometer data [TKZW08] was developed in a later work.

## 4.1. MULTILINEAR REPRESENTATION

Table 4.1: *Results for truncating technical and natural modes from our tensors filled with walking motions (using quaternions).*

| Dimension core tensor | Entries core tensor | Size core tensor in percent | Memory usage in percent | $E_{total}$ | visual rating |
|---|---|---|---|---|---|
| \multicolumn{6}{c}{Truncation of Data Mode of $\Phi_{Walk}^{f \cdot n \times a \times s \times r}$} | | | | | |
| $7140 \times 5 \times 4 \times 3$ | 428 400 | 100 % | 12 000 % | 0.0000 | excellent |
| $60 \times 5 \times 4 \times 3$ | 3 600 | 0.8403 % | 100.8520 % | 0.0000 | excellent |
| $53 \times 5 \times 4 \times 3$ | 3 180 | 0.7423 % | 89.0873 % | 0.0000 | excellent |
| $52 \times 5 \times 4 \times 3$ | 3 120 | 0.7283 % | 87.4066 % | 0.0634 | excellent |
| $50 \times 5 \times 4 \times 3$ | 3 000 | 0.7003 % | 84.0453 % | 0.2538 | very good |
| $40 \times 5 \times 4 \times 3$ | 2 400 | 0.5602 % | 67.2386 % | 1.1998 | very good |
| $30 \times 5 \times 4 \times 3$ | 1 800 | 0.4202 % | 50.4318 % | 2.1221 | very good |
| $20 \times 5 \times 4 \times 3$ | 1 200 | 0.2801 % | 33.6251 % | 3.6258 | good |
| $10 \times 5 \times 4 \times 3$ | 600 | 0.1401 % | 16.8184 % | 6.3961 | good |
| $5 \times 5 \times 4 \times 3$ | 300 | 0.0700 % | 8.4150 % | 9.3932 | satisfying |
| $4 \times 5 \times 4 \times 3$ | 240 | 0.0560 % | 6.7344 % | 10.4260 | satisfying |
| $3 \times 5 \times 4 \times 3$ | 180 | 0.0420 % | 5.0537 % | 10.9443 | sufficient |
| $2 \times 5 \times 4 \times 3$ | 120 | 0.0280 % | 3.3730 % | 11.5397 | poor |
| $1 \times 5 \times 4 \times 3$ | 60 | 0.0140 % | 1.6923 % | 11.8353 | poor |
| \multicolumn{6}{c}{Truncation of Actor Mode of $\Phi_{Walk}^{f \cdot n \times a \times s \times r}$} | | | | | |
| $60 \times 4 \times 4 \times 3$ | 2 880 | 0.6723 % | 100.6828 % | 4.3863 | satisfying |
| $60 \times 3 \times 4 \times 3$ | 2 160 | 0.5042 % | 100.5135 % | 6.4469 | satisfying |
| $60 \times 2 \times 4 \times 3$ | 1 440 | 0.3361 % | 100.3443 % | 8.2369 | satisfying |
| $60 \times 1 \times 4 \times 3$ | 720 | 0.1681 % | 100.1751 % | 10.7773 | sufficient |
| \multicolumn{6}{c}{Truncation of Style Mode of $\Phi_{Walk}^{f \cdot n \times a \times s \times r}$} | | | | | |
| $60 \times 5 \times 3 \times 3$ | 2 700 | 0.6303 % | 100.6410 % | 3.5868 | good |
| $60 \times 5 \times 2 \times 3$ | 1 800 | 0.4202 % | 100.4300 % | 5.8414 | sufficient |
| $60 \times 5 \times 1 \times 3$ | 900 | 0.2101 % | 100.2190 % | 8.5770 | poor |
| \multicolumn{6}{c}{Truncation of Repetition Mode of $\Phi_{Walk}^{f \cdot n \times a \times s \times r}$} | | | | | |
| $60 \times 5 \times 4 \times 2$ | 285 600 | 66.667 % | 100.5712 % | 2.7639 | good |
| $60 \times 5 \times 4 \times 1$ | 142 800 | 33.333 % | 100.2904 % | 5.0000 | good |
| \multicolumn{6}{c}{Truncation of Frame and DOF Mode of $\Phi_{Walk}^{f \times n \times a \times s \times r}$} | | | | | |
| $26 \times 91 \times 5 \times 4 \times 3$ | 141960 | 20.9288 % | 22.8968 % | 0.5492 | very good |
| $21 \times 91 \times 5 \times 4 \times 3$ | 114660 | 16.9040 % | 18.8020 % | 0.7418 | very good |
| $21 \times 46 \times 5 \times 4 \times 3$ | 57960 | 8.5449 % | 9.6534 % | 0.9771 | very good |
| $15 \times 34 \times 5 \times 4 \times 3$ | 30 600 | 4.5113 % | 5.3252 % | 1.9478 | good |
| $14 \times 35 \times 5 \times 4 \times 3$ | 29 400 | 4.3344 % | 5.1519 % | 1.9817 | good |
| $13 \times 37 \times 5 \times 4 \times 3$ | 28 860 | 4.2548 % | 5.0933 % | 1.9724 | good |
| $12 \times 39 \times 5 \times 4 \times 3$ | 28 800 | 4.1398 % | 4.9994 % | 1.9907 | good |

# CHAPTER 4. MOTION SYNTHESIS

Table 4.2: *Truncation results for grabbing motions (using quaternions).*

| Dimension core tensor | Entries core tensor | Size core tensor in percent | Memory usage in percent | $E_{total}$ | visual rating |
|---|---|---|---|---|---|
| Truncation of Data Mode of $\Phi_{Grab}^{f\text{-}n \times a \times s \times r}$ | | | | | |
| $8449 \times 5 \times 3 \times 3$ | 380 205 | 100 % | 18 775 % | 0.0000 | excellent |
| $60 \times 5 \times 3 \times 3$ | 2 700 | 0.7101 % | 134.0548 % | 0.0000 | excellent |
| $55 \times 5 \times 3 \times 3$ | 2 475 | 0.6510 % | 122.8845 % | 0.0000 | excellent |
| $50 \times 5 \times 3 \times 3$ | 2 250 | 0.5918 % | 111.7142 % | 0.0000 | excellent |
| $45 \times 5 \times 3 \times 3$ | 2 025 | 0.5326 % | 100.5439 % | 0.0000 | excellent |
| $40 \times 5 \times 3 \times 3$ | 1 800 | 0.4734 % | 89.3736 % | 1.2632 | very good |
| $35 \times 5 \times 3 \times 3$ | 1 575 | 0.4143 % | 78.2033 % | 2.1265 | very good |
| $30 \times 5 \times 3 \times 3$ | 1 350 | 0.3551 % | 67.0330 % | 2.9843 | very good |
| $25 \times 5 \times 3 \times 3$ | 1 125 | 0.2959 % | 55.8628 % | 3.9548 | good |
| $20 \times 5 \times 3 \times 3$ | 900 | 0.2367 % | 44.6925 % | 5.1628 | good |
| $15 \times 5 \times 3 \times 3$ | 675 | 0.1775 % | 33.5222 % | 6.6799 | satisfying |
| $10 \times 5 \times 3 \times 3$ | 450 | 0.1184 % | 22.3519 % | 8.8702 | sufficient |
| $5 \times 5 \times 3 \times 3$ | 225 | 0.0592 % | 11.1816 % | 11.5604 | sufficient |
| $4 \times 5 \times 3 \times 3$ | 180 | 0.0473 % | 8.9475 % | 12.4463 | poor |
| $3 \times 5 \times 3 \times 3$ | 135 | 0.0355 % | 6.7135 % | 12.7304 | poor |
| $2 \times 5 \times 3 \times 3$ | 90 | 0.0237 % | 4.4794 % | 13.4234 | poor |
| $1 \times 5 \times 3 \times 3$ | 45 | 0.0118 % | 2.2454 % | 13.7150 | poor |
| Truncation of DOF Mode of $\Phi_{Grab}^{f \times n \times a \times s \times r}$ | | | | | |
| $71 \times 91 \times 5 \times 3 \times 3$ | 290 745 | 76.4706 % | 80.6560 % | 0.0000 | excellent |
| $71 \times 86 \times 5 \times 3 \times 3$ | 274 770 | 72.2689 % | 76.2978 % | 0.0001 | excellent |
| $71 \times 61 \times 5 \times 3 \times 3$ | 194 895 | 51.2605 % | 54.5069 % | 0.1311 | excellent |
| $71 \times 51 \times 5 \times 3 \times 3$ | 162 945 | 42.8571 % | 45.7906 % | 0.4332 | good |
| $71 \times 41 \times 5 \times 3 \times 3$ | 130 995 | 34.4538 % | 37.0742 % | 1.0450 | satisfying |
| $71 \times 31 \times 5 \times 3 \times 3$ | 99 045 | 26.0504 % | 28.3579 % | 2.2182 | sufficient |
| $71 \times 21 \times 5 \times 3 \times 3$ | 67 095 | 17.6471 % | 19.6415 % | 3.9491 | sufficient |
| $71 \times 11 \times 5 \times 3 \times 3$ | 35 145 | 9.2437 % | 10.9252 % | 7.1531 | poor |
| $71 \times 6 \times 5 \times 3 \times 3$ | 19 170 | 5.0420 % | 6.5670 % | 10.1546 | poor |
| $71 \times 1 \times 5 \times 3 \times 3$ | 3 195 | 0.8403 % | 2.2088 % | 14.3765 | poor |

Table 4.3: *Truncation results for cartwheel motions (using quaternions).*

| Dimension core tensor | Entries core tensor | Size core tensor in percent | Memory usage in percent | $E_{total}$ | visual rating |
|---|---|---|---|---|---|
| Truncation of Data Mode of $\Phi_{Cart}^{f\text{-}n \times a \times s \times r}$ | | | | | |
| $30 \times 4 \times 3$ | 360 | 0.4002 % | 250.4279 % | 0.0000 | excellent |
| $12 \times 4 \times 3$ | 144 | 0.1601 % | 100.1879 % | 0.0000 | excellent |
| $11 \times 4 \times 3$ | 132 | 0.1467 % | 91.8412 % | 1.6780 | good |
| $10 \times 4 \times 3$ | 120 | 0.1334 % | 83.4945 % | 3.2163 | satisfying |
| $9 \times 4 \times 3$ | 108 | 0.1200 % | 75.1478 % | 5.7641 | sufficient |
| $8 \times 4 \times 3$ | 96 | 0.1067 % | 66.8012 % | 8.1549 | poor |
| $5 \times 4 \times 3$ | 60 | 0.0667 % | 41.7611 % | 13.2847 | poor |
| $1 \times 4 \times 3$ | 12 | 0.0133 % | 8.3745 % | 22.4095 | poor |

## 4.1. MULTILINEAR REPRESENTATION

Table 4.4: Computation times for PCA and N-Mode-SVD for the data used in the examples.

| Dimension Motion Matrix | Time PCA (in sec.) | Dimension Core Tensor | Time $N$-mode SVD (in sec.) |
|---|---|---|---|
| $119 \times 2280$ | 0.636 | $95 \times 119 \times 4 \times 3 \times 2$ | 5.675 |
| $95 \times 2280$ | 0.621 | $95 \times 95 \times 4 \times 3 \times 2$ | 4.968 |
| $80 \times 2280$ | 0.615 | $95 \times 80 \times 4 \times 3 \times 2$ | 4.461 |
| $5 \times 2280$ | 0.600 | $95 \times 5 \times 4 \times 3 \times 2$ | 2.295 |

## 4.2 Data-driven Texturing of Human Motions

### 4.2.1 Introduction

Creating natural looking human animations is a challenging and time-consuming task, even for skilled animators. As generating such motions manually is very costly, tools for accelerating this process are highly desirable, in particular for pre-visualization or animation involving many characters. In this work a novel method for fully automated data-driven texturing of motion data is presented. Based on a database containing a large unorganized collection of motion samples (mocap database) we are able to either

- transform a given "raw" motion according to the characteristic features of the motion clips included in the database (style transfer) or

- even complete partial animation, e.g., by adding the motion of the upper body if only legs have been previously animated (motion completion) or

- enhance a low quality motion to a natural looking, fully animated motion sequence (motion texturing).

By choosing an appropriate database different artistic goals can be achieved such as making a motion more natural or stylized. In contrast to existing approaches like the seminal work by Pullen and Bregler [PB02] our method is capable of dealing with arbitrary motion clips without manual steps, i.e. steps involving annotation, segmentation or classification. Consequently, as indicated by the examples, our technique is able to synthesize smooth transitions between different motion classes if a large mocap database is available. Finally, our synthesis yields realistic results for rough, extremely styled input even missing spatial translation over time.

### 4.2.2 Overview

The basic idea of our method is to take advantage of motion samples from large databases to improve a given motion.

## 4.2. DATA-DRIVEN TEXTURING OF HUMAN MOTIONS

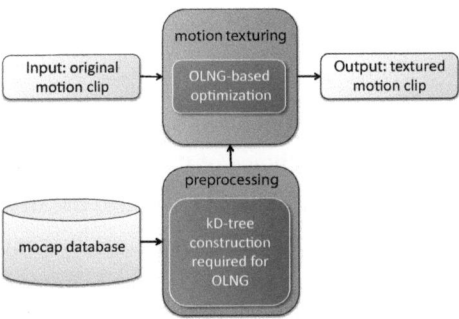

*Figure 4.10: Workflow of the proposed method for texturing of human motions.*

To achieve this end, for each frame pose of the input motion, matching motion segments of a few frames in length are retrieved from the motion capture database. For efficient retrieval a technique called Online Lazy Neighborhood Graph (OLNG) is employed, see [TZK+11] and Section 2.7. In essence this method is able to identify global temporal similarities based on local neighborhoods in pose space.

Afterwards, a new motion is synthesized using multi grid optimization techniques, based on the input and the prior information from the database. For our implementation a skeleton-based pose representation with joints and bones is assumed. However, since the method is directly applicable to other motion data (i.e. positional marker data) this constitutes no general limitation of our approach. In the following sections the individual steps of our pipeline will be discussed in more detail.

**Preprocessing**

In a preprocessing step all mocap data from the prior-database are at first normalized with respect to global position and orientation [KTWZ10]. Based on normalized positional data of all available joints we then build an efficient spatial indexing structure (kd-tree) that is required for OLNG. In addition, linear marker velocities as well as accelerations are stored. These quantities are needed for subsequent prior-based motion synthesis.

# CHAPTER 4. MOTION SYNTHESIS

## Motion synthesis

We use an energy minimization formulation which is frequently used in data driven computer animation. Our specific choice of the energy terms to be minimized most closely resembles the one used in [TZK+11]. Here, the objective function is consisting of four different terms: a control term $E_{control}$ that measures the distance of synthesized and given joint positions included in the feature set, as well as pose $E_{pose}$ and motion priors $E_{smooth}$ and $E_{motion}$ enforcing positions, acceleration and velocities of joints to be comparable to examples retrieved from the database.

$$\mathbf{x}_{best} = \underset{\mathbf{x}}{\mathrm{argmin}}(E_{pose}(\mathbf{x}) + E_{motion}(\mathbf{x}) + E_{smooth}(\mathbf{x}) + E_{control}(\mathbf{x})) \qquad (4.7)$$

The terms of this energy function are explained in more detail in the following Section 4.2.3, details on the minimization procedure are given in Section 4.2.4.

### 4.2.3 Prior Terms

During the preprocessing step linear velocities and accelerations have been computed and stored for all motion sequences included in the database.

Let $(\mathbf{y}_i)$, $i = [1..k]$ be the poses retrieved from the database by $k$-nearest-neighbor-search and $(v_i)$, $i = [1..k]$ and $(\alpha_i)$, $i = [1..k]$ the respective velocities and accelerations and let $v$ and $\alpha$ be velocity and acceleration of a given pose.

We then use kernel regression for each of the prior terms along the lines of [TZK+11]. Since the $k$-nearest-neighbor-poses were found on positional data (instead of accelerations in the original work), we are able to employ a quadratic kernel

## 4.2. DATA-DRIVEN TEXTURING OF HUMAN MOTIONS

Table 4.5: *Overview of the joints and their associated weights of our skeleton based representation.*

| ID | Name | Weight $w_j$ | ID | Name | Weight $w_j$ |
|---|---|---|---|---|---|
| 1 | root | 2.0 | 17 | head | 0.5 |
| 2 | lhipjoint | 0.0 | 18 | lclavicle | 0.5 |
| 3 | lfemur | 1.0 | 19 | lhumerus | 1.0 |
| 4 | ltibia | 2.0 | 20 | lradius | 2.0 |
| 5 | lfoot | 1.0 | 21 | lwrist | 2.0 |
| 6 | ltoes | 0.2 | 22 | lhand | 0.5 |
| 7 | rhipjoint | 0.0 | 23 | lfingers | 0.2 |
| 8 | rfemur | 1.0 | 24 | lthumb | 0.2 |
| 9 | rtibia | 2.0 | 25 | rclavicle | 0.5 |
| 10 | rfoot | 1.0 | 26 | rhumerus | 1.0 |
| 11 | rtoes | 0.2 | 27 | rradius | 2.0 |
| 12 | lowerback | 1.5 | 28 | rwrist | 2.0 |
| 13 | upperback | 1.5 | 29 | rhand | 0.5 |
| 14 | thorax | 1.5 | 30 | rfingers | 0.2 |
| 15 | lowerneck | 1.0 | 31 | rthumb | 0.2 |
| 16 | upperneck | 0.5 | | | |

function as less clusters should occur in pose space:

$$E_{\text{pose}}(\mathbf{x}) = \sum_{i=1}^{k} (\mathbf{w} \circ (\mathbf{y}_i - \mathbf{x}))^2 \qquad (4.8)$$

$$E_{\text{motion}}(\mathbf{x}) = \sum_{i=1}^{k} (\mathbf{w} \circ (v_i - v) \cdot \Delta t)^2 \qquad (4.9)$$

$$E_{\text{smooth}}(\mathbf{x}) = \sum_{i=1}^{k} (\mathbf{w} \circ (\alpha_i - \alpha) \cdot \Delta t^2)^2 \qquad (4.10)$$

with **w** denoting a vector to weight the influence of each joint of the underlying skeleton. A list of joints used in our representation and the associated weights $w_j$ is given in Table 4.5. Please note that for all above priors joint weights are considered by Hadamard vector multiplication.

## 4.2.4 Optimization procedure

The objective function (4.7) is minimized using a gradient descent approach. As we are not handling an on-line scenario in this application, it is not necessary to modify the input motion frame by frame. It is not possible to optimize complete motion sequences at once because of the resulting large number of variables. Instead we can make use of the techniques described in this section to handle whole motion sequences at once. The essential idea is to make only one optimization step for each frame, and to take into account the predecessor and successor frames. The neighbor frames are taken into account by the velocity and acceleration based motion and smoothness prior terms since both properties are computed on a window of frames.

**Multiscaling**

To improve the robustness of our method and to speed up the process of optimization, we employ a multiscale approach. This requires resampling the motion to a predefined number of lower resolutions. When the error on a certain resolution cannot be improved by at least a certain threshold (1 % in our case), the algorithm switches to the next higher resolution. Given the number of resolutions $n$ and the highest resolution $r_{max}$, we calculate lower resolutions $r_i$ by

$$r_i = \frac{r_{max}}{2^i}. \qquad (4.11)$$

For every possible scale, positions, velocities and accelerations have to be precomputed in the prior-database. Moreover, separate kd-trees have to be created. Please note that the memory requirements of the multiscale approach is bounded by twice the original data.

**Scheduling**

To improve efficiency, only a subset of all frames is considered during optimization. First this subset includes the frames with the highest associated costs. Second the predecessor and successor frames are included, since they indirectly affect synthesis

## 4.2. DATA-DRIVEN TEXTURING OF HUMAN MOTIONS

results through temporal derivatives occurring in motion and smoothness priors.

**Interleaving**

Frames that are considered to be optimized by the scheduler are optimized employing an interleaving scheme. This ensures the motion to be smoothed from both sides at discontinuous frames.

**Footprint cleanup**

To ensure footprint constraints and to avoid skating artifacts we make an additional footprint cleanup after each iteration of the optimizer. In the database all footprints were annotated using templates, according to the work of Le Callennec and Boulic [LCB06]. On the basis of the annotation of the nearest neighbors it will be decided whether there is a footprint, or not, for the current frame. If there is a footprint it is guaranteed by using an inverse kinematics algorithm.

### 4.2.5 Results

To test the effectiveness of our approach we made several tests for different scenarios that might occur in practice:

1. Motion completion: For a given motion missing joints are synthesized. In our case an animation of the lower body was used as an input to our method, and a plausible upper body motion was created (see figure 4.11).

2. Motion texturing: In this case a rough low quality motion (e.g., from interpolating few key frames) is transformed to a detailed full body animation. We transform a rough walking and jumping jack motion with stiff limbs and no root movement to a realistic full body animation (see figure 4.12).

3. Style transfer: Here, characteristic features of one individual are transferred to another within the same motion class. More precisely, we took a complex

# CHAPTER 4. MOTION SYNTHESIS

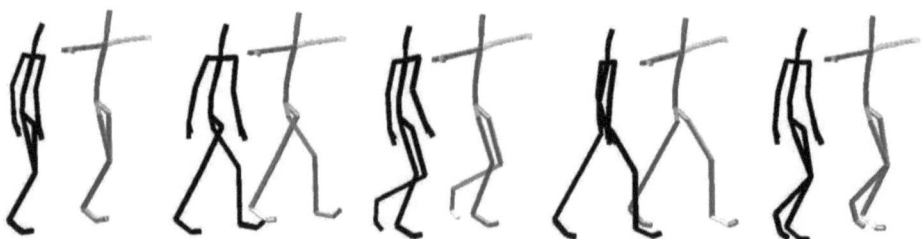

*Figure 4.11: Result for motion completion (scenario 1): Originally, the movement of the upper body was not modeled (gray stick figures). Using our technique a full body motion was synthesized (black).*

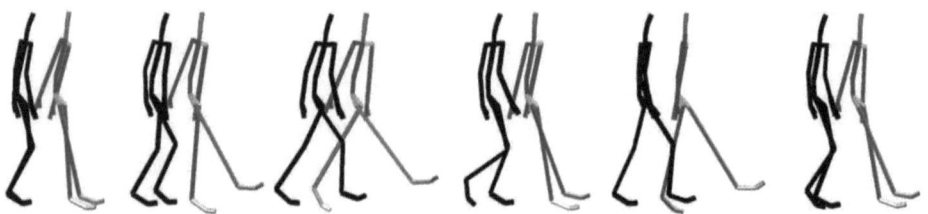

*Figure 4.12: Result for motion texturing (scenario 2): Sample frames of the original input motion showing stiff limbs and no root movement (gray stick figures). With our method a detailed full body animation was synthesized (black).*

walking sequence and adopted this motion to match the style of a different subject. This was achieved by using a database containing only motion samples from the respective subject (see figure 4.13).

All resulting motion sequences can be found in the supplemental material. We used the HDM05 database [MRC+07] for all of our examples.

The computation time for the examples presented in this section varies from three to about 90 minutes, depending on the length of the motion sequence using unoptimized MATLAB code. Most of the time is spent on optimization which can be accelerated significantly by porting to C++.

## 4.2. DATA-DRIVEN TEXTURING OF HUMAN MOTIONS

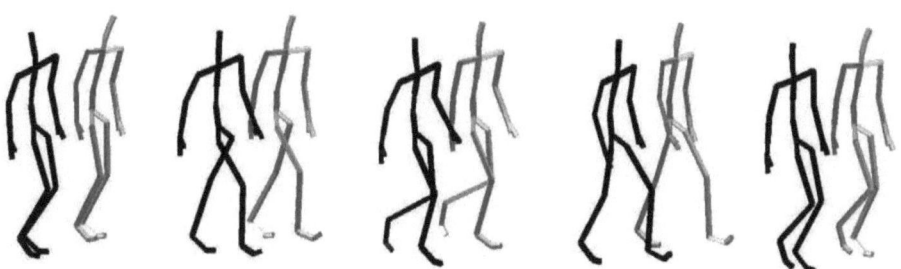

*Figure 4.13: Result for style transfer (scenario 3): An original walking motion (gray stick figures) is transformed by adopting characteristic features of another subject. The result is shown in black.*

### 4.2.6 Conclusion and Future Work

In this work a general frame-work for automated data-driven motion texturing, completion and style transfer for human motions was sketched. Our approach works reasonably well across different motion classes that previously could only be handled with massive user interaction.

Currently we define style by example motions of different subjects. However, we believe that style can not only be determined by a subject but also by other entities such as emotion, age or skill level. Exploring this idea would constitute an interesting direction of further research.

We need a mocap database containing motions which are suitable for processing a given clip according to our method. Thus, the results strongly depend on the prior information stored in the database. Investigating the impact of using different databases is of fundamental importance and requires more work.

The scenario of motion completion is a common challenge especially using low-cost capturing systems as KINECT. The integration of our algorithms into such a capturing pipeline is a topic for future research.

CHAPTER 4. MOTION SYNTHESIS

## 4.3 Dynamic Motion Graphs

In this section the so called *Dynamic Motion Graphs* (DMG) will be introduced. The goal of this section is to provide a framework for synthesis of human motion from sparse input data. The general problem, synthesizing human motions from sparse input data, can be divided if we consider the domain the input data are sparse in. In this section the input data are sparse in the temporal domain. Thus, we assume that a motion sequence to be synthesized is described by only a few key frames. The basic idea is to first construct motion graphs between subsequent key frames. Secondly, search for a candidate motion that connects all key frames. Finally, the candidate motion is improved with the motion texturing technique introduced in the previous section.

If the user is not satisfied by the result he may add additional constraints that are fulfilled after running the motion texturing procedure again. The result of these considerations is an iterative animation scheme, that allows for an interactive motion editing process. With this technique at hand it is easy to animate complex human motion sequences in a short time, compared to complete key framing, even for untrained artists. In contrast to existing motion graph approaches, we do not compute a graph in advance, but build the graph structure on the fly. The motion graph stays implicit, a fact that results in faster computation time since we do not enroll a whole precomputed graph into the environment. In contrast to prior motion synthesis approaches that base on a static nearest neighbor graph our motion graph construction does not suffer from a nearest-neighbor-search with quadratic runtime.

The next sections are organized as follows: A review of related work in this area is given in Section 4.3.1, a short overview of our method is given in Section 4.3.2, a detailed description on the construction of our dynamic motion graphs follows in Section 4.3.3 and the cleaning step is explained in more detail in Section 4.3.4. Results of this synthesis approach are given in Section 4.3.5. We conclude this chapter in Section 4.3.6.

## 4.3. DYNAMIC MOTION GRAPHS

### 4.3.1 Related Work

In recent decades, many techniques have been developed for the synthesis of natural human motions. We focus on the set of example based techniques which reuse previously recorded data for motion synthesis. Many of the methods are based on one or more of the following principles.

The first principle, *parametric synthesis*, generates motion spaces from a given set of example motion sequences. Allowing interpolation [BW95], the results can be adapted to specific spatial or temporal constraints [WH97, KG04].

The second underlying principle is the concatenation of motion segments. Short motion segments are linked together, at appropriate locations, to create one long sequence. Motion graphs [KGP02, AF02, AFO03] have become a standard technique in data-driven computer animation. They compute possible transitions between motion sequences in advance. The transitions and the corresponding motion sequences are subsequently stored in a graph structure. Motion segments are then combined according to a path through the graph, so that they meet the requirements of the user. While first works on motion graphs did not allow to interpolate between motion segments, newer extensions [SO06, HG07, SH07] combine concatenation and parametric synthesis.

These extended motion graph techniques can be divided into *Online approaches* and *Offline approaches*. Online approaches generate a motion of specific task interactive as feedback to users control. A typical example is running motion that can be controlled by a game controller [LCR$^+$02, SO06, HG07]. Offline approaches are used to generate motions under a variety of given constraints [SH07]. Thus, the underlying algorithms are more costly and not suitable to achieve interactive frame rates. Using a global optimization requires for a precomputed motion graph to find a solution. To search for such an optimal solution an $A^*$ search can be employed.

In some works [WB03, WB08], the authors attempt to find optimal transitions between motion segments. In the evaluation [RP04, LK06, RP07] of the motion graph-based methods it was found that many problems of these methods are caused by the exponential complexity of the $A^*$ based path planning in enrolled motion graphs. A problem that gets worse when more motion data are added to the graph to generate more possible transitions.

All previous approaches work on small sets of given motion capture data only. This is due to the fact that searching techniques with a quadratic runtime were used in most applications. Chai and Hodgins [CH05] use a neighbor graph, computed in a preprocessing step, on a motion database allowing for fast nearest-neighbor-search. Kovar and Gleicher [KG04] perform numerical and "logical" similarity searches on collections of motion capture data. They build so-called "match webs" on dense distance matrices that are quadratic in the size of the database. Müller et al. [MRC05] use binary geometric features and index structures to address the problem of content-based retrieval on large motion databases. Whereas the binary geometric features are well suited for defining notions of logical similarity of motions and for coming up with "motion templates" [MR06], they are not suitable in contexts requiring close numerical similarity of motions. Krüger et al. [KTWZ10] introduce a searching technique with a complexity of $k\log(n)$ where $n$ is the size of the database and $k$ is the number of nearest neighbors. They make use of numeric, medium dimensional feature sets and employ kd-trees for the $k$-nearest-neighbor-search. The authors show that this searching technique is applicable in different scenarios without loss of quality and scales well to huge databases.

In the area of online approaches Lee et al. [LWB+10] introduce *motion fields*. This interactive technique computes motion to an online control without using any motion graph like structure. Therefore a combination of nearest neighbor poses and a Markov decision process is used to compute the next frames.

Lo and Zwicker [LZ10] make use of a bidirectional search algorithm when enrolling motion graphs into the environment. Thus, the depth of search trees has been halved, which gave a huge speed advantage. For motion planning and enrolling the motion graph into the environment they employ the technique described by Lau and Kuffner [LK05, LK06]. In this work the motion capture data are put into a finite-state machine (FSM), and based on that FSM a search tree is precomputed. Since the size of the search tree grows exponentially with respect to the depth level, the amount of motion data that can be handled with this method is limited. Additionally, the user

## 4.3. DYNAMIC MOTION GRAPHS

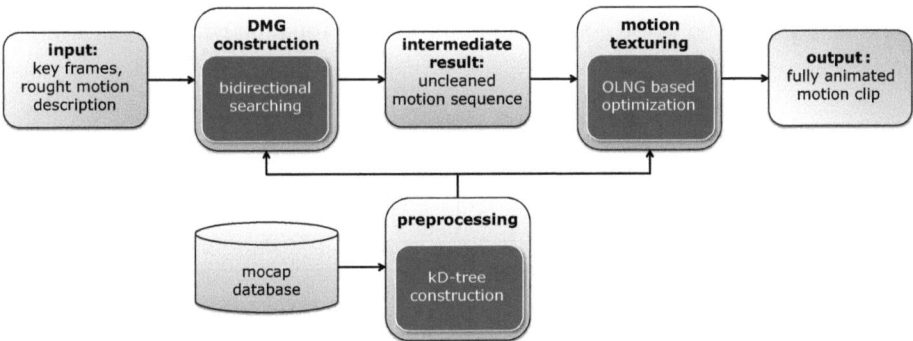

*Figure 4.14: Workflow of the proposed method for synthesizing motion sequences.*

does not have full control over the animation since this technique does not support key frames. Only points in space can be provided as constraints to describe a scene.

### 4.3.2 Overview

Our method requires a rough description of the motion to be synthesized with a few key frames as input. Based on the key frames we then search for motion segments that might start or end at the key frames. The motion segments are used to build a motion graph structure between subsequent key frames. A candidate for the resulting motion is found by a shortest path algorithm on the motion graph. We call this result *intermediate motion*. This motion might have some blending or footskating artifacts. Thus, the intermediate motion is cleaned by our motion texturing technique (see Section 4.2) to obtain the final result. See Figure 4.14 for an overview.

### 4.3.3 Motion Graph Construction

This section describes the construction of a motion graph to compute a motion sequence based on user defined key frames. In the following let $K = \{\mathbf{k}_1, \ldots, \mathbf{k}_N\}$, where $N \in \mathbb{N}$, be the description of the input motion based on $N$ key frames $\mathbf{k}_i$. The index $i$ gives information about the temporal order of the given key frames. Each key frame $\mathbf{k}$ is a vector including the position of the root node of the underlying skeleton

CHAPTER 4. MOTION SYNTHESIS

representation in the world coordinate frame and the rotational data for each joint of the skeleton:

$$\mathbf{k} = \begin{pmatrix} p_{\text{root}} \\ q_1 \\ \vdots \\ q_m \end{pmatrix}$$

The rotational degrees of freedom are represented as quaternions and the skeleton has $m = 31$ joints in our case. We construct a graph between two key frames $\mathbf{k}_i$ and $\mathbf{k}_{i+1}$ only. To obtain a motion sequence satisfying all key frames, the resulting motions for all consecutive key frames are concatenated.

**Bidirectional search**

The main idea of our bidirectional searching is to construct a tree $\mathbf{O}$ of outgoing motion segments from the first key frame $\mathbf{k}_i$ and to construct a tree $\mathbf{I}$ of incoming motion segments to the second key frame $\mathbf{k}_{i+1}$. The two trees are then connected by blending suitable outgoing and incoming motion segments. The result is a directed, acyclic graph $\mathbf{G}$. We refer to this graph as *dynamic motion graph* (DMG). This DMG can be searched for an optimal motion between the two key frames.

For all key frames given as user input we are able to search for the $k$ nearest neighbor frames included in the database. As result of this nearest neighbor search we get a ranked list $H_i = [h_{i,1}, \ldots, h_{i,k}]$ of indices of poses in the database that are regarded to be similar to the key frame $\mathbf{k}_i$. In this context we make use of the pose based similarity search introduced in Chapter 2. Similarity of poses can be parametrized by any feature set $\mathcal{F}$. We make use of the feature set $\mathcal{F}_E^{15}$ in this application.

Based on $H_i$ we get a set $O_i = \{O_{i,1}, \ldots, O_{i,k}\}$ of outgoing motion segments. We define an outgoing motion segment $O_{i,j}$ of a key frame to be the following frames of a nearest neighbor frame. Thus, an outgoing motion segment can be defined as list of indices $O_{i,j} = [h_{i,j} + 1, \ldots, h_{i,j} + M_{i,j}]$ referring to frames in the database. A set of incoming motion segments of previous frames can be defined in a similar way $\mathcal{I}_i = \{I_{i,1}, \ldots, I_{i,k}\}$ with $I_{i,j} = [h_{i,j} - M_{i,j}, \ldots, h_{i,j} - 1]$. We denote the indices of a motion segment $O_{i,j} = [o_{i,j}^1, \ldots, o_{i,j}^{M_{i,j}}]$ and the corresponding frames with

## 4.3. DYNAMIC MOTION GRAPHS

$O_i = [\mathbf{o}_{i,j}^1, \ldots, \mathbf{o}_{i,j}^{M_{i,j}}]$. $M_{i,j} \in \mathbb{N}$ defines the length in number of frames of the motion segments. We do not use a fixed length in our examples. Instead we follow a motion segment until a change in contact with the environment appears. The information on ground contacts is stored in the database.

We think of a node as a single frame and of an edge as motion sequence. At every node a transition to another motion segment is possible. We start the construction of the motion graph by setting a key frame $\mathbf{k}_i$ as root node of the tree $\mathbf{O}$ of outgoing motion segments and setting the key frame $\mathbf{k}_{i+1}$ as root node of the tree $\mathbf{I}$ of incoming motion segments. We then iterate the following steps until either the two trees can be connected, or stop the process after a fixed number of iterations.

1. *tree continuation:* Find $k$ outgoing motion segments $O$ and $k$ incoming motion segments $I$ for the $b$ best nodes of each tree. During the first iteration there are only two nodes, corresponding to the two key frames.

2. *add new nodes:* Store the end frames $[\mathbf{o}_{i,1}^{M_{i,1}}, \ldots, \mathbf{o}_{i,k}^{M_{i,k}}]$ of the outgoing segments and the start frames $[\mathbf{i}_{i,1}^1, \ldots, \mathbf{i}_{i,k}^1]$ of the incoming segments in nodes.

3. *check for connections:* Check if an edge $O_{i,j}$ of the tree $\mathbf{O}$ of outgoing segments and an edge $I_{i,j}$ of the tree $\mathbf{I}$ of incoming segments are close enough to build a connection between the two trees.

If one ore more connections between the trees are found we compute connecting edges to finalize the graph $\mathbf{G}$. This graph is then searched for a path that connects the key frames.

Before the steps of the graph construction are explained in detail, we must define a distance $D_{\text{node}}$. This distance measure is used to define the quality of all nodes in each tree. Based on that we can select the $b$ best nodes of the trees. If we consider that a node is useful for further construction if it leads to a node in the other tree, we define:

$$D_{\text{node}}(\mathbf{a}) = \underset{\mathbf{b}}{\operatorname{argmin}}\, D_{\text{pose}}(\mathbf{a}, \mathbf{b}) \qquad (4.12)$$

$\forall \mathbf{b} \in \mathbf{I}$ if $\mathbf{a} \in \mathbf{O}$ and vice versa. This definition makes use of the pose based distance:

## CHAPTER 4. MOTION SYNTHESIS

$$D_{\text{pose}}(\mathbf{a}, \mathbf{b}) = \sum_{J=1}^{31} w_J |p_J(\mathbf{a}) - p_J(\mathbf{b})| \qquad (4.13)$$

Where $w_J$ is joint weight and $p_J(\mathbf{a})$ describes the position of the $J$-th joint of the pose $\mathbf{a}$. $w$ is chosen to be one for the hands, feet and the head joint of the skeleton, and zero for all other joints. In words, $D_{\text{node}}(\mathbf{a})$ is the euclidean distance between the hands, the feet and the head of the closest node in the other tree. With this distance in hand the three steps for graph construction are now explained in more detail:

**Tree continuation:** For both trees $\mathbf{O}$ and $\mathbf{I}$ we build a priority queue, storing pointers to the nodes of the corresponding tree. The priority of the nodes is defined by the distance measure $D_{\text{pose}}$. In each iteration of the tree construction we regard only the $b$ best nodes of each tree. Thus, only branches of the trees that are heading towards the other tree are explored further. In the first iteration only the nodes that correspond to the two key frames are explored. By storing the nodes in the priority queue no nodes are discarded. If no good children are found from a node that was considered in an iteration, a node that was not considered may be regarded in a later iteration.

**Add new nodes:** For all motion segments that were regarded in an iteration we add an edge containing the motion segment and a node to the trees. The cost of an edge $E_{i,j}$ is computed as:

$$C_{\text{edge}}(E_{i,j}) = \sum_{J=1}^{31} \sum_{F=1}^{M_{i,j}} v(E_{i,j}(F, J)) \qquad (4.14)$$

where $v(E_{i,j}(F, J)$ is the velocity of the $J$-th joint at the $F$-th frame of the edge $E_{i,j}$. This cost function considers the number of frames of the motion segment as well as the distance the motion traveled in space during this time. Due to this distance function slow motions and detours will be punished.

The end frames of the outgoing motion segments and the start frames of the incoming motion segments are added as nodes to the trees. For each new node

## 4.3. DYNAMIC MOTION GRAPHS

the distance $C_{\text{edge}}$ is computed and a pointer to this node is added to one of the priority queues.

**Check for connections:** For each motion segment that is added to one of the trees we check if a connection to the other tree is possible. A connection is possible if the trees overlap in space and some edges are close enough to allow a blending between the corresponding motion segments.

First we check whether frames are close using the root-node positions. For this reason we employ spatial hashing. The main idea is to quantize the space into voxels and to use the quantized root node position of a frame to compute its hash key. All positions that are close then fall into neighboring voxels. Using hash maps, close frames in neighboring voxels can be found in constant time. During our experiments a voxelsize of 10 cm has proven to be useful.

Whenever an incoming motion segment $I_i$ is added to the tree of incoming motion segments all frames $[\mathbf{i}^i_1, \ldots, \mathbf{i}^i_M]$ are added to a hash map $\mathcal{H}_I$. All frames $[\mathbf{o}^i_1, \ldots, \mathbf{o}^i_M]$ of outgoing motion sequence then are used as a query to look for a close incoming motion segment.

In case some possible connections of the trees are found, we stop the iterative searching procedure and connect edges of the trees where possible.

**Connecting Edges**

The connection of edges converts the two trees of outgoing motion segments for key frame $\mathbf{k}_i$ and incoming segments for key frame $\mathbf{k}_{i+1}$ to a motion graph that is enrolled into the environment.

If a window of close frames in two motion segments is found, we perform a linear blending between $[\mathbf{o}^i_s, \ldots, \mathbf{o}^i_e]$ and $[\mathbf{i}^i_s, \ldots, \mathbf{i}^i_e]$, where $s$ and $e$ denote the start and end frames of the window in the incoming and outgoing motion segment. This blending is performed on the skeleton's root trajectory and on the rotational data. The blended motion segment $[\mathbf{b}_1, \ldots, \mathbf{b}_{e-s}]$ is concatenated to a new motion segment $B = [\mathbf{o}_1, \ldots, \mathbf{o}_{s-1}, \mathbf{b}_1, \ldots, \mathbf{b}_{e-s}, \mathbf{i}_{e+1}, \ldots, \mathbf{i}_M]$. The distance $D(B)$ of the motion segment $B$

# CHAPTER 4. MOTION SYNTHESIS

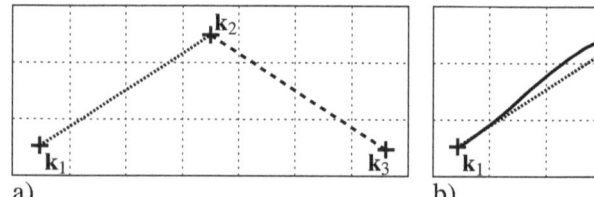

Figure 4.15: *The concatenation of motion segments (dotted and dashed) can result in discontinuities at the key frames. The cleaning step based on our motion texturing technique will give a smooth result, still respecting all given constraints.*

is computed as it is for the other motion segments. Finally a new edge is added to the graph, containing the motion segment $B$ and its associated cost $D(B)$. An example based on real data is given in Figure 4.17. This example corresponds to the walking motion that will be explained in more detail in Section 4.3.5.

**Path search and Intermediate Result**

Once a motion graph is constructed a path connecting the given keyframes **k** must be found. Our graph is directed and acyclic by construction. Thus, we can employ algorithms for directed acyclic graphs again (cf. Section 2.4.1). As an intermediate result we use the motion that is concatenated of the motion segments along the optimal path. In particular, foot skating artifacts and discontinuous motions should be adjusted.

## 4.3.4 Cleaning the Intermediate Result

Especially around the key frames the simple concatenation of motion segments can lead to discontinuous motions. This problem is illustrated in the sketch in Figure 4.15. The green and blue lines correspond to motion segments that both fulfill the key frame $k_2$. Nevertheless, the motion sequence is not continuous around that key frame. The red line is a symbol for a motion sequence that is close to the given input motion, fulfills the key frame and is continuous at the key frame. Thus, it is a

## 4.3. DYNAMIC MOTION GRAPHS

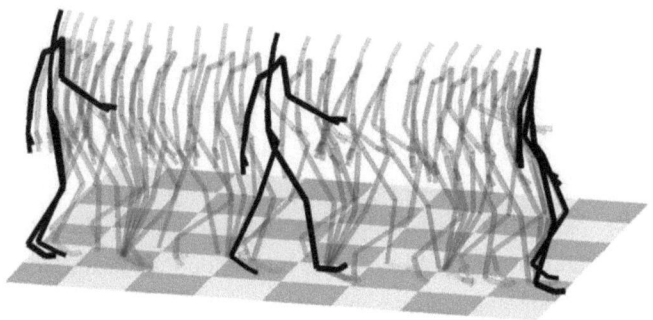

*Figure 4.16: An example for a synthesized walking sequence: Black poses were given as key frames. The poses in between (different shades of gray) were synthesized.*

desired result of the cleaning step.

The second problem that arises is that blending of motion segments can introduce foot skating artifacts. Therefore, a further processing of the motion is necessary. For this reason it is possible to employ the motion texturing algorithm introduced in Section 4.2.

In this case the concatenated result is handled as a raw input motion. Additionally, to make sure that all constraints are fulfilled, the original key frames are fixed and not allowed to be changed during this process. Therefore the frames around the key frames have to be adapted more precisely. Even if the motion is given much more detailed here, fine details can be well adapted. We refer to the result section for more details of how the cleaning process contributes to the final result.

### 4.3.5 Results

In this section we give some examples of motions synthesized with our method. In addition, certain examples are analyzed and evaluated in more depth. For all experiments presented in this section we made use of the entire HDM05 [MRC$^+$07] database and excluded the motion files from which key frames were taken.

CHAPTER 4. MOTION SYNTHESIS

**Walking Example**

The simplest specification of a scene consists of two key frames representing the start and the end of a two step walking motion. The motion from which these steps have been taken was removed from the database. The outgoing motion segments and the incoming motion segments for the two key frames are shown in Figure 4.17 a), key frame $\mathbf{k}_1$ and $\mathbf{k}_2$. Some frames from the synthetic motion are shown in Figure 4.16. In both figures an additional third key frame $\mathbf{k}_3$ is added. Thus, the resulting motions are—as expected—four step walking motions.

In Figure 4.17 b) the motion segments are shown for a scene where the key frame $\mathbf{k}_2$ was removed. Here the trees **O** and **I** had to be explored in more depth before a connection could be found. The resulting motion is a four step motion anyway. This simple example shows that on principle the concept of our motion synthesis technique is working.

**Systematic Evaluation**

To evaluate how our technique reacts to different scenes we performed two different experiments that are based on the walking motion example introduced in the previous section. Since our graph is not computed in advance, the evaluation methods proposed by Lau and Kuffner [LK06] and by Reitsma and Pollard [RP04, RP07] are not suitable for our case. These methods evaluate how many paths lead to discrete cells of the environment when enrolling the precomputed motion graph. Instead we sample the environment by moving a key frame $\mathbf{k}_2$ while key frame $\mathbf{k}_1$ stays fixed. To evaluate how the DMG reacts to the given scenes we regarded the following properties of the resulting motion sequences:

1. The length in frames of the resulting motion sequences. A good motion should be as short as possible according the construction and the distances of the dynamic motion graph.

2. The cost $C_{\text{edge}}$ for the complete final motion sequence.

## 4.3. DYNAMIC MOTION GRAPHS

The movement of $k_2$ can be done in different ways, two are described and evaluated in more detail in the following paragraphs:

**Rotate second key frame**  For this experiment the second key frame was rotated around the upward pointing y-axis at its original position. We computed motions from the first key frame to the second one, where the second key frame was rotated by ten degree steps. A picture of the key frame $k_1$ and the rotated copies of ke frame $k_2$ is given in Figure 4.18 a), while Figure 4.18 b) shows the trajectories of the root nodes for all resulting motion sequences. Our algorithm found a solution for all given key frames $k_2$. The length in frames and the cost $C_{edge}$ are visualized in Figure 4.19. As expected motions to key frames that have slightly been rotated have the same length as the non-rotated version. Key frames rotated in higher degrees lead to longer motion sequences. An interesting detail: rotations between 80 and 130 degrees as well as rotation between 300 and 320 degrees lead to longer motion sequences than rotation between 140 and 290 degrees. This fact can be explained by the structure of the database: If no appropriate turning motion is included the resulting motion has a detour to go. Regarding the results for the cost function it shows similar properties as the number of frames. Thus, the change of the rotation angle does not influence the speed of the motions leading to the key frame.

**Move second key frame**  To create test scenes in this experiment the position and orientation of the second key frame $k_2$ was modified. First the whole motion sequence was translated so that the first frame was moved to the y-axis. Then the two key frames were extracted. The second key frame was translated such that the distance varied from 0.5 to 1.5 times the original distance in 0.2 steps. Additionally we rotated the second key frame by 30 degree steps around the global y-axis. This corresponds to a rotation around the first key frame $k_1$ in the selected distance. In Figure 4.20 a) all key frames are shown. The first key frame is drawn in black color, the translated and rotated copies of the second one are drawn in shades of gray. We computed motion sequences for all created scenes. For each of these key frame combinations a motion sequence was found using the proposed method. For evaluation we regarded the same properties as for the first experiment. The results are visualized in Figure 4.21. Here the number of frames and the value of $C_{\text{edge}}$ are visualized. The shortest motion clips result from the second key frames that were translated but not rotated. They correspond to walk to different distances on a line. Here again motions that have to get to a key frame that was rotated around 90 degrees or 270 and 300 degrees need detours to reach the goal. Appropriate motions also seem not to be included in the database. In this experiment some more differences between the number of frames and the cost function were found. The overall structure of both diagrams seems to be similar, but there are slight differences. Regarding the motions in the 0 degree axis, they seem to have a similar number of frames but having an increasing cost. Since the motions have the same length but are traveling different distances in space they have to do this with a higher velocity. Similar changes in speed of the motions can be found for other differences, too. For example, some of the resulting motion sequences along the 90 degree axis have a high number of frames while their cost value is only medium. When regarding these motions, one can see that they are partly standing at a point and are turning slowly before they are able to continue walking towards the second key frame.

**Large Synthetic Examples**

We computed several examples by extracting a set of key frames from motion capture recordings taken from the HDM05 database [MRC$^+$07]. Every two seconds a key frame was extracted. The motion sequence from which the key frames were taken was deleted from the database. For results we refer to the video in the supplemental material.

**Evaluation of the Cleaning Step**

We show the effect of the cleaning step on the basis of the walking example introduced before. In this simple example the problems described already arise. In Figure 4.22 a) the y-position of the skeletons root node is plotted for the intermediate motion (black line) and the final result (gray line). The black dashed lines represent time points at which a key frame is fulfilled. The intermediate motion shows some artifacts around frames 18, 40 and 60. After the cleaning step the root trajectory is more smooth; a desired result. Please note that some extrema (frames 30 and 70) are more strongly pronounced in the final result. A result that could not be obtained by applying a simple filtering technique.

Figure 4.22 b) shows the absolute velocities of the right foot for the same motion sequences. Here, we can identify two phases where the foot is having ground contact between frames 20 and 40 and between frames 60 and 80. The intermediate motion has a strong foot skating artifact around frame 75. This as well as the blending artifacts is cleaned by our motion texturing technique.

### 4.3.6 Conclusion and Future Work

In this section a technique for generating motion sequences from a few key frames was introduced. We can handle challenging cases including different styles of motions and large spatial distances between key frames. The systematic evaluation of our motion synthesis procedure shows that we are able to compute motion sequences for key frames that are distributed differently in the scene.

Currently we search the database for incoming and outgoing motion sequences. These original motion capture sequences are later modified by blending, inverse kinematics and the cleaning step. In contrast to interpolated motion graph approaches we do not extend a precomputed motion graph with interpolated motion sequences. This strategy ensures fast synthesis with diverse motion classes but allows to modify the motion capture data anyway.

Nevertheless, we believe that allowing frame wise interpolations, like it is done in the work of Lee et al. [LWB+10], in combination with our searching and cleaning techniques might result in motion sequences that take shorter tours in the environment.

Employing a frame wise interpolation requires a sophisticated distance function. In the original work a Markov Decision Process is used in combination with reinforcement learning. The given cost function is a local one and can not be used to

## CHAPTER 4. MOTION SYNTHESIS

plan a motion between two given key frames.

The integration into a commercial animation system, like 3dsMax, Maya, Lightwave or Blender, and tests of these implementation by skilled animators, is one topic for future work. Their comments would be helpful in designing more appropriate techniques than the existing ones.

The influence of the underlying database is not only interesting for the cleaning step, but also important for the bidirectional search. We assume that the more motions are included in the database, the better results can be obtained by our method. An assumption that has to be proved in later research.

## 4.3. DYNAMIC MOTION GRAPHS

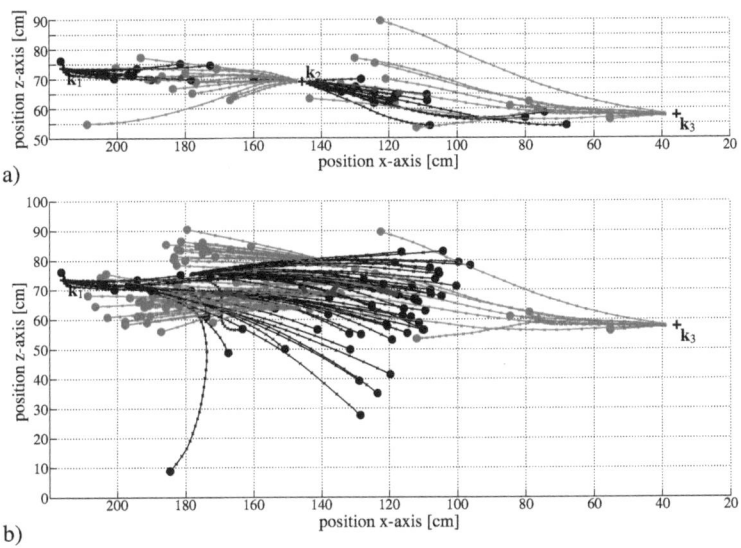

Figure 4.17: Examples for edge connection based on real data (top view): To the given key frames $\mathbf{k}_1, \mathbf{k}_2, \mathbf{k}_3$ outgoing motion segments (black) and incoming motion segments (gray) were found. The frames along the motion segments are represented by crosses, the nodes at the beginning of incoming sequences and at the end of outgoing sequences are drawn as circles. The bold gray lines represent possible connections of close frames. The motion sequence in a) was sketched using three key frames, while the sequence in b) was sketched using two key frames. In b) more iterations were needed until connections of the two trees were found. In this example only the four best nodes of the incoming and outgoing segments were regarded for continuation.

## CHAPTER 4. MOTION SYNTHESIS

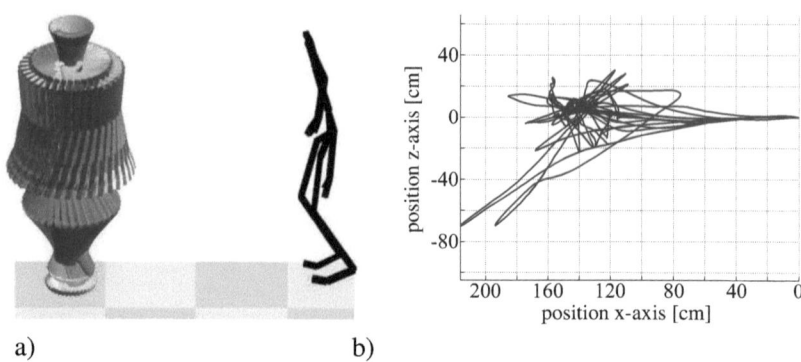

Figure 4.18: a) Key frames used for the first experiment. Key frame $k_1$ is drawn red, the rotated versions of the second key frame $k_2$ are drawn in shades of gray. b) Top view on the root trajectories of the resulting motion sequences.

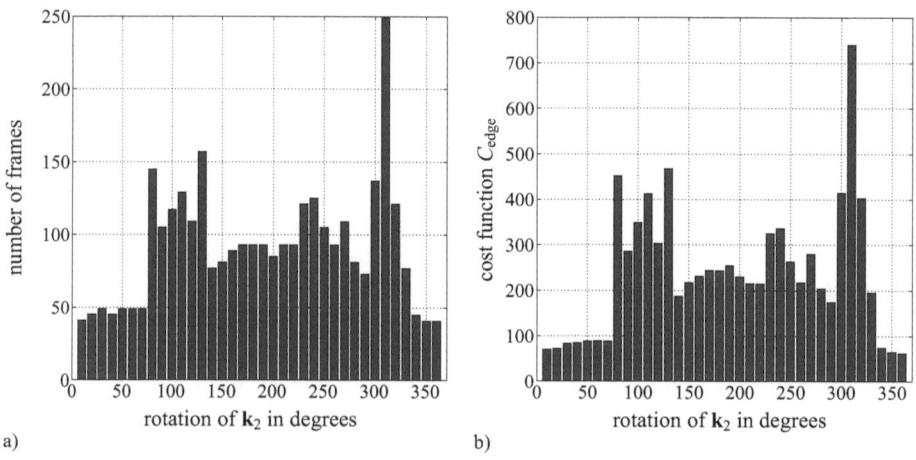

Figure 4.19: Results for the experiments rotating the second key frame $k_2$. a) Number of frames of the resulting motion sequences. b) Values of the cost function $C_{\text{edge}}$.

## 4.3. DYNAMIC MOTION GRAPHS

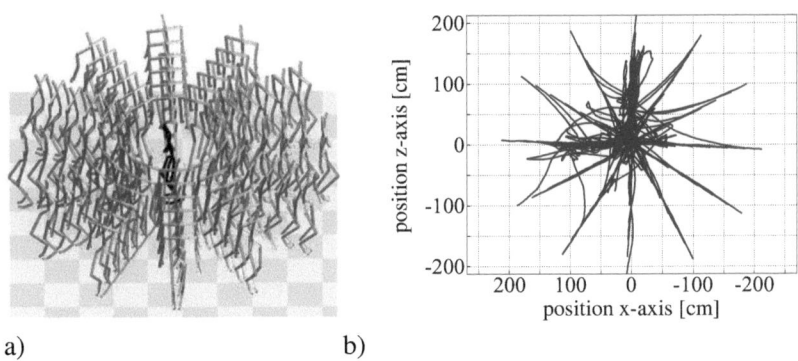

Figure 4.20: a) Key frames used for the second experiment. Key frame $k_1$ is drawn in red, the rotated and translated versions of the second key frame $k_2$ are drawn from green to blue. b) Top view on the root trajectories of the resulting motion sequences.

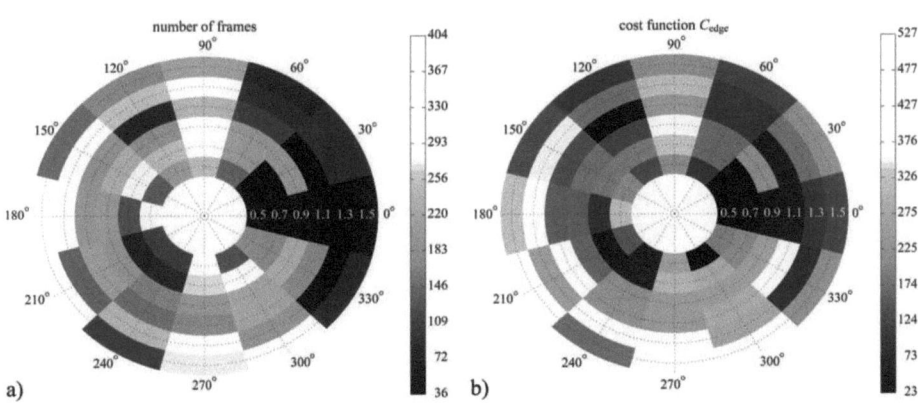

Figure 4.21: Results for the experiment where the second key frame was moved: a) Number of frames of the resulting motion sequences. b) Value of the cost function $C_{\text{edge}}$.

# CHAPTER 4. MOTION SYNTHESIS

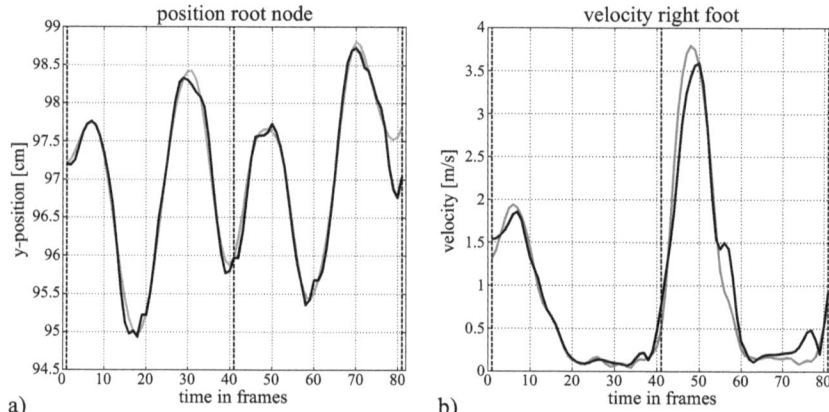

Figure 4.22: a) Position of the root node for an intermediate walking motion (black) and the final motion after the cleanup step (gray). The dashed lines indicate key frame positions. b) Velocity of the right foot for the same walking sequences.

*"Sure as I am breathing*
*Sure as I'm sad*
*I'll keep this wisdom in my flesh*
*I leave here believing more than I had*
*And there's a reason I'll be*
*A reason I'll be back"*

Eddie Vedder – No Ceiling

# 5

# Conclusion and Future Work

## 5.1 Conclusion

In this thesis several techniques and algorithms to handle motion capture data were presented. As was shown, efficient similarity search is of fundamental importance for fast, high quality motion synthesis. Using the lazy neighborhood graph presented in Chapter 2 we are able to search databases with logarithmic complexity in the size of the underlying database. We also showed that the proposed local and global similarity searches improve different applications.

The multilinear representation of motion capture data can be used for fast motion synthesis since only a few multiplications are needed to construct a motion sequence. Examples of this synthesis are presented in Section 4.1. With this technique for motion synthesis in hand we were able to annotate unknown motion capture documents employing an analysis by synthesis approach in Chapter 3. The multilinear representation has a rigid structure and does not scale well if one wants to consider multiple

CHAPTER 5. CONCLUSION AND FUTURE WORK

motion classes. Thus, this representation can only be used in some well defined scenarios.

More general tools for motion synthesis were introduced with the motion texturing technique in Section 4.2 and the dynamic motion graphs in Section 4.3. Both techniques are based on our fast similarity search. Thus, we are able to construct local models based on the nearest neighbors taken from a huge database. With the help of the DMG we can synthesize motion sequences based on sparse key frames. The effectiveness of this approach was shown in some systematic evaluations and large scenes based on many key frames.

## 5.2 Future Work

In this work physical properties of human motions were only considered as part of feature sets. These feature sets were used for dynamic time warping or for the fast similarity search. All motion synthesis approaches introduced in this thesis only work on the kinematic level. To perform the synthesis of motion sequences on physics based layer is one topic of future research. A physics based layer is also needed when data-driven techniques should be combined with controller based ones.

The extension from a pose based neighborhood search to a global search, based on the lazy neighborhood graph (LNG) contains information on the temporal evolution of the motion sequences. Using this temporal context one could study the local dimension of the motion capture data, based on principal component analysis, for example. This research can give an interesting view on the dimensionality of human motions.

Based on the LNG search and its online version, the OLNG, an anticipation of the evolution in time of a stream of motion data can be done. This prediction might be useful for the motion planning of robots, or reactive virtual characters. First experiments in this direction show interesting results. To use adapted variants of the LNG for other types of data will be another topic of future research.

# Bibliography

[AF02]  ARIKAN, Okan ; FORSYTH, D. A.: Interactive motion generation from examples. In: *SIGGRAPH '02: Proceedings of the 29th annual conference on Computer graphics and interactive techniques*. San Antonio, Texas : ACM Press, 2002. – ISBN 1–58113–521–1, S. 483–490 95

[AFO03]  ARIKAN, Okan ; FORSYTH, David A. ; O'BRIEN, James F.: Motion synthesis from annotations. In: *ACM Trans. Graph.* 22 (2003), July, 402–408. http://dx.doi.org/10.1145/882262.882284. – DOI 10.1145/882262.882284. – ISSN 0730–0301 15, 25, 34, 45, 95

[AI08]  ANDONI, Alexandr ; INDYK, Piotr: Near-optimal hashing algorithms for approximate nearest neighbor in high dimensions. In: *Commun. ACM* 51 (2008), Nr. 1, S. 117–122. http://dx.doi.org/10.1145/1327452.1327494. – DOI 10.1145/1327452.1327494. – ISSN 0001–0782 13

[ALP06]  ABE, Y. ; LIU, C.K. ; POPOVIĆ, Z.: Momentum-based parameterization of dynamic character motion. In: *Graphical Models* 68 (2006), Nr. 2, S. 194–211 35

[Ari06]  ARIKAN, Okan: Compression of motion capture databases. In: *ACM Trans. Graph.* 25 (2006), Nr. 3, S. 890–897. http://dx.doi.org/10.1145/1141911.1141971. – DOI 10.1145/1141911.1141971. – ISSN 0730–0301. – SIGGRAPH 2006 63

# BIBLIOGRAPHY

[BA00]     BRO, Rasmus ; ANDERSSON, Claus A.: *The N-way Toolbox for MATLAB.* http://www.models.kvl.dk/nwaytoolbox/. Version: 2000 67

[BBK01]    BÖHM, Christian ; BERCHTOLD, Stefan ; KEIM, Daniel A.: Searching in high-dimensional spaces: Index structures for improving the performance of multimedia databases. In: *ACM Comput. Surv.* 33 (2001), Nr. 3, 322–373. http://dx.doi.org/10.1145/502807.502809. – DOI 10.1145/502807.502809. – ISSN 0360–0300 10, 12

[BCPP08]   BEAUDOIN, P. ; COROS, S. ; PANNE, M. van d. ; POULIN, P.: Motion-Motif Graphs. In: GROSS, M. (Hrsg.) ; JAMES, D. (Hrsg.): *ACM SIGGRAPH/Eurographics Symposium on Computer Animation*, 2008 13, 14, 25

[BE09]     BASTEN, B. J. H. ; EGGES, A.: Evaluating distance metrics for animation blending. In: *FDG '09: Proceedings of the 4th International Conference on Foundations of Digital Games.* New York, NY, USA : ACM, 2009. – ISBN 978–1–60558–437–9, S. 199–206 13

[BH00]     BRAND, Matthew ; HERTZMANN, Aaron: Style machines. In: *Proc. ACM SIGGRAPH 2000*, ACM Press, 2000 (Computer Graphics Proc.). – ISBN 1–58113–208–5, S. 183–192 45

[BKZW11a]  BAUMANN, Jan ; KRÜGER, Björn ; ZINKE, Arno ; WEBER, Andreas: Data-Driven Completion of Motion Capture Data. In: *Workshop on Virtual Reality Interaction and Physical Simulation (VRIPHYS)*, 2011 39

[BKZW11b]  BAUMANN, Jan ; KRÜGER, Björn ; ZINKE, Arno ; WEBER, Andreas: Filling Long-Time Gaps of Motion Capture Data. In: *SCA'11: Poster Proc. ACM SIGGRAPH/Eurographics Symposium on Computer Animation*, 2011 39

[BMS08]    BAAK, Andreas ; MÜLLER, Meinard ; SEIDEL, Hans-Peter: An Efficient Algorithm for Keyframe-based Motion Retrieval in the Presence of

Temporal Deformations. In: *Proceeding of the 1st ACM international conference on Multimedia information retrieval* ACM, 2008. – ISBN 978–1–60558–303–7, S. 451–458 44, 46, 49

[BSP+04] BARBIČ, Jernej ; SAFONOVA, Alla ; PAN, Jia-Yu ; FALOUTSOS, Christos ; HODGINS, Jessica K. ; POLLARD, Nancy S.: Segmenting motion capture data into distinct behaviors. In: HEIDRICH, Wolfgang (Hrsg.) ; BALAKRISHNAN, Ravin (Hrsg.): *Proceedings of the Graphics Interface 2004 Conference*, Canadian Human-Computer Communications Society, 2004. – ISBN 1–56881–227–2, 185–194 46, 63

[BW95] BRUDERLIN, Armin ; WILLIAMS, Lance: Motion signal processing. In: COOK, Robert (Hrsg.): *Proceedings of the 22nd annual conference on Computer graphics and interactive techniques*, ACM Press, New York, 1995. – ISBN 0–80791–701–4, 97–104 54, 64, 68, 95

[Car04] CARNEGIE MELLON UNIVERSITY GRAPHICS LAB: *CMU Motion Capture Database.* http://mocap.cs.cmu.edu. Version: 2004 11, 45, 50

[CH05] CHAI, Jinxiang ; HODGINS, Jessica K.: Performance animation from low-dimensional control signals. In: *ACM Trans. Graph.* 24 (2005), July, 686–696. http://dx.doi.org/10.1145/1073204.1073248. – DOI 10.1145/1073204.1073248. – ISSN 0730–0301 12, 13, 14, 15, 31, 32, 45, 63, 82, 96

[CH07] CHAI, Jinxiang ; HODGINS, Jessica K.: Constraint-based Motion Optimization Using A Statistical Dynamic Model. In: *ACM Transactions on Graphics* 26 (2007), Nr. 3. – SIGGRAPH 2007 38, 63

[CHP07] COOPER, Seth ; HERTZMANN, Aaron ; POPOVIĆ, Zoran: Active learning for real-time motion controllers. In: *ACM Trans. Graph.* 26 (2007), Nr. 3, S. 5. http://dx.doi.org/10.1145/1276377.1276384. – DOI 10.1145/1276377.1276384. – ISSN 0730–0301 45

BIBLIOGRAPHY

[CLRS01] CORMEN, T. H. ; LEISERSON, C. E. ; RIVEST, R. L. ; STEIN, C.: *Introduction to Algorithms*. MIT Press, 2001 27

[EMMT04] EGGES, A. ; MOLET, T. ; MAGNENAT-THALMANN, N.: Personalised real-time idle motion synthesis. In: *12th Pacific Conference on Computer Graphics and Applications (PG 2004)*, 2004, S. 121–130 13

[EMWZ05] EFFENBERG, Alfred ; MELZER, Joachim ; WEBER, Andreas ; ZINKE, Arno: MotionLab Sonify: A Framework for the Sonification of Human Motion Data. In: *Ninth International Conference on Information Visualisation (IV'05)*. London, UK : IEEE Press, Juli 2005. – ISBN 0–7695–2397–8, S. 17–23 82

[Fal96] FALOUTSOS, C.: *Searching Multimedia Databases by Content*. Springer, 1996 http://www.cs.cmu.edu/~christos/mybookInfo.html 12

[FF05] FORBES, Kate ; FIUME, Eugene: An efficient search algorithm for motion data using weighted PCA. In: *Proc. 2005 ACM SIGGRAPH/Eurographics Symposium on Computer Animation*, ACM Press, 2005. – ISBN 1–7695–2270–X, S. 67–76 45, 63

[FHP07] FALOUTSOS, Christos ; HODGINS, Jessica ; POLLARD, Nancy: Database techniques with motion capture. In: *SIGGRAPH '07: ACM SIGGRAPH 2007 courses*. San Diego, California : ACM, 2007, S. 1 13

[GBT04] GLARDON, Pascal ; BOULIC, Ronan ; THALMANN, Daniel: PCA-Based Walking Engine Using Motion Capture Data. In: *CGI '04: Proceedings of the Computer Graphics International (CGI'04)*. Washington, DC, USA : IEEE Computer Society, 2004. – ISBN 0–7695–2171–1, S. 292–298 63

[GP00] GIESE, Martin A. ; POGGIO, Tomaso: Morphable Models for the Analysis and Synthesis of Complex Motion Patterns. In: *International*

## BIBLIOGRAPHY

*Journal of Computer Vision* 38 (2000), Nr. 1, 59-73. http://www.springerlink.com/content/vw5g1624504m3npu/ 45, 63, 64, 68

[HG07] HECK, Rachel ; GLEICHER, Michael: Parametric motion graphs. In: *I3D '07: Proceedings of the 2007 symposium on Interactive 3D graphics and games*. New York, NY, USA : ACM Press, 2007. – ISBN 978–1–59593–628–8, S. 129–136 12, 25, 38, 95

[HJBC05] HILDENBRAND, D. ; J., Zamora ; BAYRO-CORROCHANO, E.: Inverse kinematics computation in computer graphics and robotics using conformal geometric algebra. In: *International Conference on Clifford Algebras and their Applications*, 2005 15

[HMF07] HUNT, W. ; MARK, W. R. ; FUSSELL, D.: Fast and lazy build of acceleration structures from scene hierarchies. In: *IEEE Symposium on Interactive Ray Tracing (RT '07)*, 2007, S. 47–54 38

[HPP05] HSU, Eugene ; PULLI, Kari ; POPOVIĆ, Jovan: Style translation for human motion. In: *ACM Trans. Graph.* 24 (2005), Nr. 3, S. 1082–1089. http://dx.doi.org/10.1145/1073204.1073315. – DOI 10.1145/1073204.1073315. – ISSN 0730–0301. – SIGGRAPH 2005 64

[KBAW11] KRÜGER, Björn ; BAUMANN, Jan ; ABDALLAH, Mohammad ; WEBER, Andreas: A Study On Perceptual Similarity of Human Motions. In: *Workshop on Virtual Reality Interaction and Physical Simulation (VRIPHYS)*, 2011. – accepted for publication 39

[KG03] KOVAR, Lucas ; GLEICHER, Michael: Flexible Automatic Motion Blending with Registration Curves. In: BREEN, D. (Hrsg.) ; LIN, M. (Hrsg.): *Eurographics/SIGGRAPH Symposium on Computer Animation*, Eurographics Association, 2003, 214-224 64, 68

[KG04] KOVAR, Lucas ; GLEICHER, Michael: Automated extraction and parameterization of motions in large data sets. In: *ACM Transactions*

## BIBLIOGRAPHY

>*on Graphics* 23 (2004), Nr. 3, 559–568. http://doi.acm.org/10.
>1145/1015706.1015760. – ISSN 0730–0301. – SIGGRAPH 2004
>10, 12, 14, 15, 25, 26, 30, 45, 63, 82, 95, 96

[KGP02] KOVAR, Lucas ; GLEICHER, Michael ; PIGHIN, Frédéric: Motion Graphs. In: *ACM Transactions on Graphics* 21 (2002), Nr. 3, 473–482. http://doi.acm.org/10.1145/566654.566605. – ISSN 0730–0301. – SIGGRAPH 2002 10, 12, 25, 45, 55, 56, 63, 95

[KPZ+04] KEOGH, Eamonn ; PALPANAS, Themistoklis ; ZORDAN, Victor B. ; GUNOPULOS, Dimitrios ; CARDLE, Marc: Indexing large human-motion databases. In: *VLDB '04: Proceedings of the Thirtieth international conference on Very large data bases*, VLDB Endowment, 2004. – ISBN 0–12–088469–0, S. 780–791 10, 13, 45

[KTMW08] KRÜGER, Björn ; TAUTGES, Jochen ; MÜLLER, Meinard ; WEBER, Andreas: Multi-Mode Tensor Representation of Motion Data. In: *Journal of Virtual Reality and Broadcasting* (2008) 43, 44, 46, 53, 54, 56

[KTW07] KRÜGER, Björn ; TAUTGES, Jochen ; WEBER, Andreas: Multi-Mode Representation of Motion Data. In: BRAZ, J. (Hrsg.) ; VAZQUEZ, P.-P. (Hrsg.) ; MADEIRAS PEREIRA, J. (Hrsg.): *The 2nd International Conference on Computer Graphics Theory and Applications (GRAPP 2007)*. Barcelona, Spain : INSTICC Press, März 2007. – ISBN 978–972–8865–72–6, S. 21–29 44

[KTWZ10] KRÜGER, Björn ; TAUTGES, Jochen ; WEBER, Andreas ; ZINKE, Arno: Fast Local and Global Similarity Searches in Large Motion Capture Databases. In: *Proceedings of the 2010 ACM SIGGRAPH/Eurographics Symposium on Computer Animation*. Aire-la-Ville, Switzerland, Switzerland : Eurographics Association, Juli 2010 (SCA '10), 1–10 87, 96

# BIBLIOGRAPHY

[LCB06]   LE CALLENNEC, Beno ; BOULIC, Ronan: Robust Kinematic Constraint Detection for Motion Data. In: *Proceedings of ACM SIGGRAPH / Eurographics Symposium on Computer Animation*, 2006 91

[LCR+02]   LEE, Jehee ; CHAI, Jinxiang ; REITSMA, Paul S. A. ; HODGINS, Jessica K. ; POLLARD, Nancy S.: Interactive control of avatars animated with human motion data. In: *SIGGRAPH '02: Proceedings of the 29th annual conference on Computer graphics and interactive techniques*. San Antonio, Texas : ACM Press, 2002. – ISBN 1–58113–521–1, S. 491–500 10, 15, 95

[Lev96]   LEVA, P. de: Adjustments to Zatsiorsky-Seluyanov's segment inertia parameters. In: *Journal of Biomechanics* 29 (1996), Nr. 9, S. 1223–1230 34

[LK05]   LAU, Manfred ; KUFFNER, James J.: Behavior Planning for Character Animation. In: *2005 ACM SIGGRAPH / Eurographics Symposium on Computer Animation*, 2005, S. 271–280 96

[LK06]   LAU, Manfred ; KUFFNER, James J.: Precomputed search trees: planning for interactive goal-driven animation. In: *SCA '06: Proceedings of the 2006 ACM SIGGRAPH/Eurographics symposium on Computer animation*. Vienna, Austria : Eurographics Association, 2006. – ISBN 3–905673–34–7, S. 299–308 95, 96, 104

[LP02]   LIU, C. K. ; POPOVIĆ, Zoran: Synthesis of complex dynamic character motion from simple animations. In: *SIGGRAPH '02: Proceedings of the 29th annual conference on Computer graphics and interactive techniques*. New York, NY, USA : ACM, 2002. – ISBN 1–58113–521–1, S. 408–416 35

[LS02]   LEE, Jehee ; SHIN, Sung Y.: General Construction of Time-Domain Filters for Orientation Data. In: *IEEE Transactions*

121

BIBLIOGRAPHY

on *Visualizatiuon and Computer Graphics* 8 (2002), Nr. 2, 119–128. http://csdl.computer.org/comp/trans/tg/2002/02/v0119abs.htm. – ISSN 1077–2626 74

[LWB+10]  LEE, Yongjoon ; WAMPLER, Kevin ; BERNSTEIN, Gilbert ; POPOVIĆ, Jovan ; POPOVIĆ, Zoran: Motion fields for interactive character locomotion. In: *ACM Trans. Graph.* 29 (2010), Dezember, 138:1–138:8. http://dx.doi.org/10.1145/1882261.1866160. – DOI 10.1145/1882261.1866160. – ISSN 0730–0301 39, 96, 107

[LZ10]  Lo, Wan-Yen ; ZWICKER, Matthias: Bidirectional Search for Interactive Motion Synthesis. In: *Computer Graphics Forum* 29 (2010), Nr. 2, S. 563–573 96

[LZWM05]  LIU, Guodong ; ZHANG, Jingdan ; WANG, Wei ; MCMILLAN, Leonard: A system for analyzing and indexing human-motion databases. In: *Proc. 2005 ACM SIGMOD Intl. Conf. on Management of Data*, ACM Press, 2005. – ISBN 1–59593–060–4, S. 924–926 45, 63

[MA06]  MOUNT, David M. ; ARYA, Sunil: ANN: A Library for Approximate Nearest Neighbor Searching / Department of Computer Science. Version: 2006. http://www.cs.umd.edu/~mount/ANN/. University of Maryland, College Park, Maryland, U.S.A., 2006. – Programming Manual 17

[MBS09]  MÜLLER, Meinard ; BAAK, Andreas ; SEIDEL, Hans-Peter: Efficient and Robust Annotation of Motion Capture Data. In: *Proceedings of the ACM SIGGRAPH/Eurographics Symposium on Computer Animation*, 2009, S. 17–26 44, 46, 47, 48

[MK06]  MUKAI, Tomohiko ; KURIYAMA, Shigeru: Multilinear Motion Synthesis Using Geostatistics. In: *ACM SIGGRAPH / Eurographics Symposium on Computer Animation - Posters and Demos*, 2006, S. 21–22 63, 67

# BIBLIOGRAPHY

[MP07]  McCann, James ; Pollard, Nancy: Responsive Characters from Motion Fragments. In: *ACM Transactions on Graphics* 26 (2007), Nr. 3. – SIGGRAPH 2007 12, 25

[MR06]  Müller, Meinard ; Röder, Tido: Motion Templates for Automatic Classification and Retrieval of Motion Capture Data. In: *SCA '06: Proceedings of the 2006 ACM SIGGRAPH/Eurographics Symposium on Computer Animation*, ACM Press, 2006, S. 137–146 12, 43, 44, 45, 46, 47, 68, 82, 96

[MRC05]  Müller, Meinard ; Röder, Tido ; Clausen, Michael: Efficient content-based retrieval of motion capture data. In: *ACM Trans. Graph.* 24 (2005), July, 677–685. http://dx.doi.org/10.1145/1073204.1073247. – DOI 10.1145/1073204.1073247. – ISSN 0730–0301 12, 43, 45, 46, 82, 96

[MRC+07]  Müller, Meinard ; Röder, Tido ; Clausen, Michael ; Eberhardt, Bernhard ; Krüger, Björn ; Weber, Andreas: Documentation: Mocap Database HDM05 / Universität Bonn. Version: june 2007. http://www.mpi-inf.mpg.de/resources/HDM05. 2007 (CG-2007-2). – Computer Graphics Technical Report. – ISSN 1610–8892 11, 45, 50, 73, 92, 103, 106

[Mül07]  Müller, Meinard: *Information Retrieval for Music and Motion*. Springer, 2007. – ISBN 978–3–540–74047–6 25, 28, 43, 44, 46, 47, 54

[MW03]  Myers, Jerome L. ; Well, Arnold D.: *Research design and statistical analysis*. Mahwah, N.J. : Lawrence Erlbaum Associates, 2003 18

[MYHW08]  Meng, J. ; Yuan, J. ; Hans, M. ; Wu, Y.: Mining Motifs from Human Motion. In: Mania, K. (Hrsg.) ; Reinhard, E. (Hrsg.): *Eurographics 2008 – Short Papers*, 2008, S. 71–74 13, 28

# BIBLIOGRAPHY

[MZF06]  MAJKOWSKA, Anna ; ZORDAN, Victor B. ; FALOUTSOS, Petros: Automatic Splicing for Hand and Body Animations. In: *ACM SIGGRAPH / Eurographics Symposium on Computer Animation*, 2006. – ISBN 3-905673-34-7, S. 309–316 63, 64

[Nar96]  NARDELLI, E.: Distributed *k*-d trees. In: *Proceedings 16th Conference of Chilean Computer Science Society (SCCC '96)*, 1996, S. 142–154 38

[OBHK05]  ORMONEIT, Dirk ; BLACK, Michael J. ; HASTIE, Trevor ; KJELLSTRÖM, Hedvig: Representing cyclic human motion using functional analysis. In: *Image Vision Comput.* 23 (2005), Nr. 14, S. 1264–1276 63

[PB02]  PULLEN, Katherine ; BREGLER, Christoph: Motion capture assisted animation: texturing and synthesis. In: *ACM Trans. Graph.* 21 (2002), July, 501–508. http://dx.doi.org/10.1145/566654.566608. – DOI 10.1145/566654.566608. – ISSN 0730–0301 45, 86

[RCB98]  ROSE, Charles ; COHEN, Michael F. ; BODENHEIMER, Bobby: Verbs and adverbs: multidimensional motion interpolation. In: *IEEE Comput. Graph. Appl.* 18 (1998), Nr. 5, S. 32–40. http://dx.doi.org/10.1109/38.708559. – DOI 10.1109/38.708559. – ISSN 0272–1716 45

[RCO05]  ROVSHAN, Kalanov ; CHO, Jieun ; OHYA, Jun: D-12-79 A Study of Synthesizing New Human Motions from Sampled Motions Using Tensor Decomposition. In: *Proceedings of the IEICE General Conference* 2005 (2005), Nr. 2, 229. http://ci.nii.ac.jp/naid/110004746409/en/ 63

[RM05]  RÖBER, Niklas ; MASUCH, Maic: Playing Audio-only Games: A compendium of interacting with virtual, auditory Worlds. In: *Proceedings of Digital Games Research Conference*. Vancouver, Canada, 2005 82

[RP04]  REITSMA, P. S. A. ; POLLARD, N. S.: Evaluating motion graphs for character navigation. In: *SCA '04: Proceedings of the 2004 ACM*

## BIBLIOGRAPHY

*SIGGRAPH/Eurographics symposium on Computer animation*. Aire-la-Ville, Switzerland, Switzerland : Eurographics Association, 2004. – ISBN 3–905673–14–2, S. 89–98 95, 104

[RP07] REITSMA, Paul S. A. ; POLLARD, Nancy S.: Evaluating motion graphs for character animation. In: *ACM Trans. Graph.* 26 (2007), Nr. 4, S. 18. http://dx.doi.org/10.1145/1289603.1289609. – DOI 10.1145/1289603.1289609. – ISSN 0730–0301 95, 104

[RW03] ROBBINS, K. L. ; WU, Q.: Development of a Computer Tool for Anthropometric Analyses. In: VALAFAR, Faramarz (Hrsg.) ; VALAFAR, Homayoun (Hrsg.): *Proceedings of the International Conference on Mathematics and Engineering Techniques in Medicine and Biological Sciences (METMBS'03)*. Las Vegas, USA : CSREA Press, jun 2003. – ISBN 1–932415–04–1, S. 347–353 69

[SH05] SAFONOVA, Alla ; HODGINS, Jessica K.: Analyzing the physical correctness of interpolated human motion. In: VICTOR ZORDAN, Demetri T. (Hrsg.): *SCA '05: Proceedings of the 2005 ACM SIGGRAPH/Eurographics symposium on Computer animation*. New York, NY, USA : ACM Press, 2005. – ISBN 1–59593–198–8, S. 171–180 35, 64

[SH07] SAFONOVA, Alla ; HODGINS, Jessica K.: Construction and Optimal Search of Interpolated Motion Graphs. In: *ACM Transactions on Graphics* 26 (2007), Nr. 3. – SIGGRAPH 2007 12, 25, 38, 63, 95

[SHP04] SAFONOVA, Alla ; HODGINS, Jessica K. ; POLLARD, Nancy S.: Synthesizing physically realistic human motion in low-dimensional, behavior-specific spaces. In: *ACM Transactions on Graphics* 23 (2004), Nr. 3, 514–521. http://doi.acm.org/10.1145/1015706.1015754. – ISSN 0730–0301. – SIGGRAPH 2004 13, 14, 63, 78

# BIBLIOGRAPHY

[SO06]  SHIN, Hyun J. ; OH, Hyun S.: Fat graphs: constructing an interactive character with continuous controls. In: *SCA '06: Proceedings of the 2006 ACM SIGGRAPH/Eurographics symposium on Computer animation*. Aire-la-Ville, Switzerland : Eurographics Association, 2006. – ISBN 3–905673–34–7, S. 291–298 12, 25, 33, 95

[SP05]  SULEJMANPAĆIĆ, Adnan ; POPOVIĆ, Jovan: Adaptation of performed ballistic motion. In: *ACM Trans. Graph.* 24 (2005), Nr. 1, S. 165–179. http://dx.doi.org/10.1145/1037957.1037966. – DOI 10.1145/1037957.1037966. – ISSN 0730–0301. – SIGGRAPH 2005 35

[TGB00]  TOLANI, Deepak ; GOSWAMI, Ambarish ; BADLER, Norman I.: Real-time inverse kinematics techniques for anthropomorphic limbs. In: *Graph. Models Image Process.* 62 (2000), Nr. 5, S. 353–388. – ISSN 1077–3169 13, 15

[TKZW08]  TAUTGES, Jochen ; KRÜGER, Björn ; ZINKE, Arno ; WEBER, Andreas: Reconstruction of Human Motions Using Few Sensors. In: SCHUMANN, Marco (Hrsg.) ; KUHLEN, Torsten (Hrsg.): *Virtuelle und Erweiterte Realität – 5. Workshop der GI-Fachgruppe VR/AR*. Magdeburg, Germany : Shaker-Verlag, September 2008. – ISBN 978–3–8322–7572–3, S. 1–12. – Preis für besten Beitrag (Inhalt und Präsentation) 82

[Tro02]  TROJE, Nikolaus F.: Decomposing biological motion: A framework for analysis and synthesis of human gait patterns. In: *Journal of Vision* 2 (2002), Nr. 5, S. 371–387 63

[TZK+11]  TAUTGES, Jochen ; ZINKE, Arno ; KRÜGER, Björn ; BAUMANN, Jan ; WEBER, Andreas ; HELTEN, Thomas ; MÜLLER, Meinard ; SEIDEL, Hans-Peter ; EBERHARDT, Bernd: Motion reconstruction using sparse accelerometer data. In: *ACM Trans. Graph.* 30 (2011), May, 18:1–18:12. http://dx.doi.org/10.1145/1966394.1966397. – DOI 10.1145/1966394.1966397. – ISSN 0730–0301 37, 42, 87, 88

# BIBLIOGRAPHY

[Vas02] VASILESCU, M. Alex O.: Human motion signatures: Analysis, synthesis, recognition. In: *Proc. Int. Conf. on Pattern Recognition*. Quebec City, Canada, 2002, S. 456–460 63, 67, 68

[VBPP05] VLASIC, Daniel ; BRAND, Matthew ; PFISTER, Hanspeter ; POPOVIĆ, Jovan: Face transfer with multilinear models. In: *ACM Trans. Graph.* 24 (2005), Nr. 3, S. 426–433. http://dx.doi.org/10.1145/1073204.1073209. – DOI 10.1145/1073204.1073209. – ISSN 0730–0301. – SIGGRAPH 2005 53, 56, 63, 65, 67, 68, 82

[WB03] WANG, Jing ; BODENHEIMER, Bobby: An evaluation of a cost metric for selecting transitions between motion segments. In: *SCA '03: Proceedings of the 2003 ACM SIGGRAPH/Eurographics symposium on Computer animation*. Aire-la-Ville, Switzerland, Switzerland : Eurographics Association, 2003. – ISBN 1–58113–659–5, S. 232–238 15, 95

[WB08] WANG, Jing ; BODENHEIMER, Bobby: Synthesis and evaluation of linear motion transitions. In: *ACM Trans. Graph.* 27 (2008), Nr. 1, S. 1–15. http://dx.doi.org/10.1145/1330511.1330512. – DOI 10.1145/1330511.1330512. – ISSN 0730–0301 15, 95

[WCYL03] WU, M.-Y. ; CHAO, S.P. ; YANG, S.N. ; LIN, H.C.: Content-Based Retrieval for Human Motion Data. In: *16th IPPR Conf. on Computer Vision, Graphics and Image Processing*, 2003, S. 605–612 45

[WH97] WILEY, Douglas J. ; HAHN, James K.: Interpolation Synthesis of Articulated Figure Motion. In: *IEEE Comput. Graph. Appl.* 17 (1997), Nr. 6, S. 39–45. http://dx.doi.org/10.1109/38.626968. – DOI 10.1109/38.626968. – ISSN 0272–1716 95

[ZM06] ZINKE, Arno ; MAYER, Dessislava: Iterative Multi Scale Dynamic Time Warping / Universität Bonn. Version: 2006. http://cg.cs.

# BIBLIOGRAPHY

uni-bonn.de/publications/publication.asp?id=283. 2006 (CG-2006-1). – Technical Report 71

# i want morebooks!

Buy your books fast and straightforward online - at one of world's fastest growing online book stores! Environmentally sound due to Print-on-Demand technologies.

Buy your books online at
## www.get-morebooks.com

Kaufen Sie Ihre Bücher schnell und unkompliziert online – auf einer der am schnellsten wachsenden Buchhandelsplattformen weltweit! Dank Print-On-Demand umwelt- und ressourcenschonend produziert.

Bücher schneller online kaufen
## www.morebooks.de

VDM Verlagsservicegesellschaft mbH
Heinrich-Böcking-Str. 6-8   Telefon: +49 681 3720 174   info@vdm-vsg.de
D - 66121 Saarbrücken      Telefax: +49 681 3720 1749   www.vdm-vsg.de

Printed by Books on Demand GmbH, Norderstedt / Germany